Lesson Plans for Classroom Teachers

Fifth and Sixth Grades

Robert P. Pangrazi
Arizona State University

Allyn and Bacon
Boston · London · Toronto · Sydney · Tokyo · Singapore

ISBN 0-205-19365-X

Printed in the United States of America

10 9 8 7 6 5 4 3 2   01 00 99

Library of Congress Cataloging-in-Publication Data

Pangrazi, Robert P.
    Lesson plans for classroom teachers. Fifth and sixth grades /
Robert P. Pangrazi.
        p.   cm.
    ISBN 0-205-19365-X (pbk.)
    1. Physical education for children. 2. Sports--Study and teaching
(Elementary) 3. Fifth grade (Education)--Curricula. 4. Sixth grade
(Education)--Curricula.   I. Title.
GV443.P3443 1996
372.'86043--dc21
                                                              96-46299
                                                              CIP

Lesson Plans for the School Year
Fifth Grade and Sixth Grade

WEEK	INTRODUCTORY ACTIVITY	FITNESS DEVELOPMENT ACTIVITY	LESSON FOCUS ACTIVITY	GAME ACTIVITY	PAGE
1	Move and Freeze on Signal	Teacher Leader Exercises	Orientation	Back to Back Whistle Mixer	1
2	Fastest Tag in the West	Teacher-Leader Exercises	Soccer Skills(1)	Soccer Lead-Up Games	3
3	Move and Freeze	Teacher-Leader Exercises	Soccer Skills(2)	Soccer Lead-Up Games	6
4	Popcorn	Hexagon Hustle	Soccer Skills(3)	Soccer Lead-Up Games	9
5	Run, Stop, and Pivot	Hexagon Hustle	Rhythmic Movement(1)	Triplet Stoop Pacman	11
6	European Running	Hexagon Hustle	Rhythmic Movement(2)	Cageball Target Throw Chain Tag	14
7	Hospital Tag	Circuit Training	Racquet Sport Skills	Volley Tennis One Wall Racquetball	17
8	Medic Tag	Circuit Training	Football Skills(1)	Football Lead-Up Games	19
9	Agility Run	Circuit Training	Football Skills(2)	Football Lead-Up Games	22
10	Stretching	Jogging	Walking and Jogging Skills	Recreational Activities	25
11	Stretching	Jogging	Cross-Country Running/Walking	Recreational Activities	26
12	Partner Over and Under	Exercises to Music	Individual Rope Jumping Skills(1)	Right Face One Base Tagball	27
13	Move and Manipulate	Exercises to Music	Frisbee Skills	Frisbee Keep Away Frisbee Golf	30
14	New Leader	Exercises to Music	Hockey Skills(1)	Hockey Lead-Up Games	32
15	Group Over and Under	Exercises to Music	Hockey Skills(2)	Hockey Lead-Up Games	35
16	Four Corner Sport Movement	Astronaut Drills	Basketball Skills(1)	Basketball Lead-Up Games	37
17	Dribble and Pivot	Astronaut Drills	Basketball Skills(2)	Basketball Lead-Up Games	40
18	Leapfrog	Astronaut Drills	Basketball Skills(3)	Basketball Lead-Up Games	43
19	Jog and Stretch	Aerobic Fitness	Recreational Activities	Recreational Activities	45

WEEK	INTRODUCTORY ACTIVITY	FITNESS DEVELOPMENT ACTIVITY	LESSON FOCUS ACTIVITY	GAME ACTIVITY	PAGE
20	Barker's Hoopla	Aerobic Fitness	Gymnastics (1)	Star Wars Flag Chase	46
21	Following Activity	Parachute Fitness	Gymnastics (2)	Team Handball Octopus Bomb the Pins	50
22	High Fives	Parachute Fitness	Gymnastics (3)	Pin Knockout Over the Wall	54
23	Rubber Band	Parachute Fitness	Gymnastics (4)	Octopus Fast Pass	57
24	Moving to Music	Parachute Fitness	Manipulative Skills Using Wands and Hoops	Jollyball Circle Touch Galactic Empire and Rebels	59
25	Vanishing Beanbags	Partner Aerobic Fitness and Resistance Exercises	Volleyball Skills(1)	Volleyball Lead-Up Games	62
26	Marking	Partner Aerobic Fitness and Resistance Exercises	Volleyball Skills(2)	Volleyball Lead-Up Games	65
27	Move and Perform Athletic Movements	Partner Aerobic Fitness and Resistance Exercises	Rhythmic Movement(3)	Whistle Ball More Jump the Shot Variations	67
28	Popcorn	Continuity Drills	Rhythmic Movement(4)	Scooter Kickball Touchdown Chain Tag	70
29	Move, Exercise on Signal	Continuity Drills	Juggling Skills	Bomb the Pins Pacman	73
30	Hospital Tag	Continuity Drills	Relay Activities	Relaxation Activities	75
31	Stretching	Jogging	Track and Field Skills(1)	Shuttle/Circular Relays One on One Contests	78
32	Stretching	Jogging	Track and Field Skills(2)	Shuttle/Circular Relays One on One Contests	81
33	Stretching	Jogging	Track and Field Skills(3)	Shuttle/Circular Relays One on One Contests	83
34	Personal Choice	Squad Leader Exercises with Task Cards	Long Rope Jumping Skills	Cageball Target Throw Sunday	84

WEEK	INTRODUCTORY ACTIVITY	FITNESS DEVELOPMENT ACTIVITY	LESSON FOCUS ACTIVITY	GAME ACTIVITY	PAGE
35	Personal Choice	Squad Leader Exercises with Task Cards	Softball Skills(1)	Softball Lead-Up Games	86
36	Personal Choice	Squad Leader Exercises with Task Cards	Softball Skills(2)	Softball Lead-Up Games	89

Using The Lesson Plans

The lesson plans provide a guide for presenting movement experiences in a sequential and well-ordered manner. The series of plans serve as a comprehensive curriculum. Lessons can be modified and shaped to meet the needs of individual teachers. Many teachers take activities from the lesson plans and write them on 4" by 6" note cards. All lesson presentations should be mentally rehearsed to prevent excessive use of written notes. Lesson plan note cards help relieve the burden of trying to remember the proper sequence of activities and the worry of forgetting key points of instruction.

Grade Levels

Three sets of lesson plans are available to cover the Kindergarten through sixth grade curriculum. The following is a brief description about the content included in each set of lesson plans:

Kindergarten through Second Grade. Learner characteristics of children in grades K-2 dictate the need for an enjoyable and instructional learning environment. By stressing the joy of physical activity, positive behaviors are developed that last a lifetime. The majority of activities for younger children are individual in nature and center on learning movement concepts through theme development. Children learn about basic movement principles and educational movement themes are used to teach body identification and body management skills.

Third Grade through Fourth Grade. Activities for children in this age group focus on refinement of fundamental skills and the introduction of specialized sport skills. Visual-tactile coordination is enhanced by using a variety of manipulative skills. Children should be allowed the opportunity to explore, experiment, and create activities without fear. While not stressing conformity, children need to absorb the how and also the why of activity patterns. Cooperation with peers is important as more emphasis is placed on group and team activities. Initial instruction in sport skills begins at this level and a number of lead-up activities are utilized so youngsters can apply newly learned skills in a small group setting.

Fifth Grade through Sixth Grade. Physical education instruction moves toward specialized skills and sport activities. Football, basketball, softball, track and field, volleyball, and hockey are added to the sport offerings. Students continue learning and improving sport skills while participating in cooperative sport lead-up games. Less emphasis is placed on movement concept activities and a larger percentage of instructional time is devoted to manipulative activity. Adequate time is set aside for the rhythmic program and for the program area involving apparatus, stunts, and tumbling. At this level, increased emphasis is placed on physical fitness and developmental activities. Organized and structured fitness routines are offered so that students can begin to make decisions about personal approaches to maintaining fitness levels.

Format of the Lesson Plans

Each lesson plan is divided into four instructional parts and contains enough activities for a week of instruction. Briefly, the four instructional parts of the lesson plan and major purposes of each section are as follows:

Introductory Activity: Introductory activities change weekly and are used to physiologically prepare children for activity when entering the gymnasium or activity area. Activities used in this section demand little instruction and allow time for practicing class management skills.

Fitness Development Activity: Fitness activities take 7 to 8 minutes of a 30 minute lesson. The activities should be personalized, progressive in nature, and exercise all parts of the body. Allied to the workout should be brief discussions about the values of fitness for a healthy lifestyle. A comprehensive discussion of fitness principles, fitness activities, and instructional guidelines is found in Chapter 8 of the textbook.

Lesson Focus Activities: The purpose of the lesson focus is to teach children major program objectives such as the development of eye-hand coordination, body management competency, and fundamental and specialized skills (e.g., folk dancing, shooting a basket, and catching an object). The lesson focus uses 15-20 minutes of the daily lesson depending on the length of the teaching period. Lesson focus activities are organized into units and vary in length depending on the developmental level of children. Lesson focus activities are changed weekly except when continuity of instruction demands longer units. Enough activities are placed in each lesson focus section to accommodate three to four teaching periods.

The content in each lesson is organized in a developmental sequence, with the first activity being the easiest and the last activity the most difficult. Usually, instruction starts with the first activity and proceeds forward regardless of developmental level. The implications are twofold: This progression ensures that each unit begins with success, since all children are capable of performing the beginning activities. It also assures that a proper sequence of activities will be followed during instruction. Obviously, developmentally mature children will progress further along the continuum of activities than less capable children.

Game Activity: This part of the lesson plan takes place at the closing of the lesson, utilizing the last 5-7 minutes of the period. Games are often used as a culminating activity for practicing skills emphasized in the lesson focus. In other lessons, games are unrelated to the lesson focus and are presented for the purpose of completing the lesson with a fun and enjoyable activity. The game should leave children with positive feelings so they look forward with anticipation to the next lesson. If the lesson has been physically demanding, a less active game can be played and vice versa. In some cases, a low key, relaxing activity might be chosen so that children can unwind before returning to the classroom.

Contents of the Lesson Plans

Objectives and required equipment are listed at the top of each lesson plan. This establishes the reason for teaching the lesson and makes it easy to prepare the equipment for instruction. The contents of the lesson plans is placed into two columns:

Instructional Activities: This column lists activities that will be taught in the lesson. The content in this column offers progression and sequence for activities that will be presented during the week. All activities are explained in detail and can be presented easily from each lesson plan.

Teaching Hints: This section provides points for efficient organization of the class and important learning cues. Emphasis in this column is on teaching for quality of movement rather than quantity.

Lesson Plans for Grades 5-6 - Week 1
Orientation and Class Management Activities

Objectives:
To learn and follow basic management activities necessary for participation in
    physical education classes

Equipment Required:
Tom-tom
Tape player and music for fitness
    challenges

Instructional Activities	Teaching Hints

Orientation Instructional Procedures

The first week of school should be used to teach students the system you are going to use throughout the year. The following are reminders you might find useful in establishing your expectations and routines.

1. Establish rules and expectations. Discuss your expectations with the class to assure students understand reasons for your guidelines. Explain what the consequences are when rules are not followed. Show where time-out boxes are located and how they will be used.

2. Explain to the class the method you will use to learn names. It might be helpful to ask classroom teachers to have students put their name on a piece of masking tape (name tag). Tell students that you will ask them their name on a regular basis until it is learned.

3. Develop entry and exit behaviors for students coming and leaving physical education classes. Students should know how to enter the instructional area and to leave equipment alone until told to use it. If squads are used for instruction, place students into squads and practice moving into formation on signal.

4. Decide how excuses for non-participation will be handled. If possible, set up a routine where the school nurse determines which students are excused for health reasons.

5. Safety is important. Children should receive safety rules to be followed on apparatus and playground equipment. Safety procedures to be followed in physical education classes should be discussed.

6. Illustrate how you will stop and start the class. In general, a whistle (or similar loud signal) and a raised hand is effective for stopping the class. A voice command should be used to start the class. Telling the class when before what (Chapter ??) will assure they do not begin before instructions are finished.

7. Discuss the issue, distribution, and care of equipment. Make students responsible for acquiring a piece of equipment and returning it at the end of the lesson. Place equipment around the perimeter of the teaching area to reduce the chance of students fighting over a piece of equipment.

8. Explain to the class that the format of the daily lesson will include an introductory activity, fitness development, lesson focus, and finish with a game activity.

9. Practice various teaching formations such as open-squad formation and closed-squad formation. Practice moving into a circle while moving (fall-in). Transitions between formations should be done while moving, i.e., jogging from scatter formation into a circular formation.

10. Refer to Chapter 4 and 5 in the text for detailed information about planning, developing an effective learning environment, and class management strategies.

Introductory Activity -- Move and Freeze on Signal

Have students move throughout the area using a variety of locomotor movements. On signal (whistle), they quickly freeze. Try to reduce the response latency by reinforcing students who stop quickly on signal.

The primary objective is to teach students the importance of moving under control (without bumping others or falling down) and quickly freezing.

Fitness Development Activity -- Teacher Leader Exercises

Emphasis should be placed on starting the fitness activities at a level where all students can feel successful.

Arm Circles	30 seconds
Push-Up Challenges	30 seconds
Bend and Twist	30 seconds
Treadmill	30 seconds
Sit-Up Challenges	30 seconds
Single-Leg Crab Kick	30 seconds
Knee to Chest Curl	30 seconds
Run in Place	30 seconds
Standing Hip Bend	30 seconds

Walk or jog for 3 minutes.

Tape alternating segments of silence (10 seconds) to signal a change of exercise and music to signal the duration of exercise (30 seconds).

See text, p. 163-167 for descriptions of challenges.

See text, p. 174-186 for descriptions of exercises.

Workloads should be moderate with emphasis on success for all youngsters.

Lesson Focus – Orientation

Since much time during the first week is used for orientation procedures and management, no lesson focus activity is scheduled.

Game Activity -- Management Games

Play one or two management games to teach students how to move into partner and small group formation

Back to Back

Supplies: None

Skills: Fundamental locomotor movements

Students move under control throughout the area using a variety of locomotor movements. On signal, each child stands back to back (or toe to toe) with another child. If one child ends up without a partner, the teacher takes this student as a partner. Youngsters who do not find a partner nearby run to a designated spot in the center of the area. This helps assure that students do not run around looking for a partner or feel left out. Students who move to the center spot quickly find a partner and move out of the area (to avoid crowding around the center spot). Emphasis should be placed finding a partner near them, not searching for a friend, and taking a different partner each time.

Whistle Mixer

Supplies: None

Skills: All basic locomotor movements

Children are scattered throughout the area. To begin, they move in any direction they wish. The teacher whistles a number of times in succession and raises the same number of fingers above their head to signal the group size. Children then form small groups with the number in each group equal to the number of whistles. For example, if there are four short whistles, children form circles of four--no more, no less. The goal is to find the correct number of students as quickly as possible. As soon as a group has the desired number, they sit down to signal that other may not join the group. Children who cannot find a group nearby should move to the center of the area and raise their hands to facilitate finding others without a group.

Lesson Plans for Grades 5-6 - Week 2
Soccer Skills (1)

Objectives:
To strike a ball with a variety of body parts
To dribble a ball with the feet
To trap a with a variety of body parts
To play a soccer lead-up activity and understand the joy of participation

Equipment Required:
8" foam rubber or junior soccerball for each student
Music tape for exercises
Pinnies (optional)
Cones for marking the drill areas and goals

Instructional Activities	Teaching Hints

Introductory Activity -- Fastest Tag in the West

All students are it. On signal, they try to tag each other. If they are tagged, they must freeze, but they are eligible to tag other students who pass near them. If two or more players tag each other simultaneously, they are both/all "frozen."

The idea of the game is to get all students involved in activity. Restart the game often rather than waiting for all students to be tagged.

Fitness Development Activity -- Teacher Leader Exercises

Encourage youngsters to do the best they can within the specified time limit.

Arm Circles	30 seconds
Push-Up Challenges	30 seconds
Bend and Twist	30 seconds
Treadmill	30 seconds
Sit-Up Challenges	30 seconds
Single-Leg Crab Kick	30 seconds
Knee to Chest Curl	30 seconds
Run in Place	30 seconds
Standing Hip Bend	30 seconds

Conclude the routine with 2-4 minutes of jogging, rope jumping or other aerobic activity.

Youngsters are not required to do the same workload. Children differ and their ability to perform fitness workloads differs. Make fitness a personal challenge.

Tape alternating segments of silence (10 seconds) to signal a change of exercise and music to signal the duration of exercise (30 seconds).

See text, p. 163-167 for descriptions of challenges.

See text, p. 174-186 for descriptions of exercises.

Lesson Focus -- Soccer Skills (1)

Skills
Practice the following skills:
1. Dribbling
   Dribbling is moving the ball with a series of taps or pushes to cover ground and still retain control. It allows a player to change direction quickly and to avoid opponents. The best contact point is the inside of the foot, but the outside of the foot will be used at faster running speeds. The ball should be kept close to the player to maintain control.
2. Inside-of-the-Foot Pass (Push Pass)
   The inside-of-the-foot pass is used for accurate passing over distances of up to 15 yards. Because of the technique used, this pass is sometimes referred to as the push pass. The nonkicking foot is placed well up, alongside the ball. As the kicking foot is drawn back, the toe is turned out. During the kick, the toe remains turned out so that the inside of the foot is perpendicular to the line of flight. The sole is kept parallel to the ground. At contact, the knee of the kicking leg should be well forward, over the ball, and both knees should be slightly bent.
3. Inside-of-the-Foot Trap
   This is the most common method of control, and is used when the ball is either rolling along the ground or bouncing up to knee height. The full surface of the foot, from heel to toe, should be presented perpendicular to the ball.

Contact the ball with the inside, outside, or instep of the foot.

Keep the ball near the body so it can be controlled. (Don't kick it too far in front of the body.) Dribble the ball with a controlled tap.

Place the nonkicking foot alongside the ball. Keep the head down and eyes focused on the ball during contact.

When trapping, move in line with the path of the ball and reach with the foot to meet the ball. Give when ball contact is made to absorb force.

3

4. Goalkeeping

Goalkeeping involves stopping shots by catching, stopping, or otherwise deflecting the ball. Goalkeepers should become adept at catching low rolling balls, diving on rolling balls, catching airborne balls at waist level and below, and catching airborne balls at waist height and above.

Goalkeepers should practice catching low rolling balls by getting down on one knee, with their body behind the ball to act as a backstop, and catching the ball with both hands, fingers pointing toward the ground.

Drills Using Four or More Players

Use the following partner drills to practice the skills above. Drills for four or more players should be organized so that a rotation gives all players an equal opportunity to practice skills.

1. Dribbling. Two teams of four players are lined up and facing each other about 10 yards apart. Each player at the front of the team has a ball. Both front players dribble to the center, where they exchange balls and continue dribbling to the other side. The next players perform similarly.

A variation is to have the two players meet at the center, exchange balls, and dribble back to their starting point. Action should be continuous.

2. Shooting, goalkeeping, and defense. A shooting drill against defense can be run with four players and a 15-foot goal set off with cones or other markers. One player has the ball. He advances and attempts to maneuver around a second player so that he can shoot past the goalkeeper guarding a goal. A fourth player acts as the retriever. Rotate positions.

Use foam rubber balls for goalkeeping drills to avoid hurting someone with the ball.

3. Dribbling. Four or five players, each with a ball, form a line. A "coach" stands about 15 yards in front of the line. Each player, in turn, dribbles up to the coach, who indicates with a thumb in which direction the player should dribble past. The coach should give the direction at the last possible moment.

Make sure all students get a chance to be the "coach."

4. Passing, controlling, and defense. Four players stand in the four corners of a square, 10 yards on a side. Two defensive players are inside the square. The corner players stay in place within the square and attempt to pass the ball among themselves, while the two defenders attempt to recover the ball. After a period of time, another two players take over as defenders.

This is a traditional game of keepaway using soccer balls. Encourage students to avoid body contact.

Play the soccer lead-up games after sufficient time has been allotted for skills and drills.

Game Activity - Soccer Lead-Up Games

Dribblerama

Supplies: One soccer ball for each player

Skills: Dribbling, protecting the ball

The playing area is a large circle or square, clearly outlined. All players dribble within the area. The game is played on two levels.

Level 1: Each player dribbles throughout the area, controlling the ball so that it does not touch another ball. If a touch occurs, both players go outside the area and dribble counterclockwise around the area. Once youngsters have completed dribbling one lap of the counterclockwise path, they may reenter the game.

Level 2: While dribbling and controlling the ball, each player attempts to kick any other ball out of the area. When a ball is kicked out, the player owning that ball takes it outside and dribbles around the area. Play continues until only two or three players who have not lost control of their ball are left. These are declared the winners. Bring all players back into the game and repeat.

Sideline Soccer

Supplies: A soccer ball, four cones, pinnies (optional)

Skills: Most soccer skills, competitive play

The teams line up on the sidelines of the rectangle. Three or four active players from each team are called from the end of the team line. These players remain active until a point is scored; then they rotate to the other end of the line.

The object is to kick the ball between cones that define the scoring area. The active players on each team compete against each other, aided by their teammates on the sidelines.

To start play, a referee drops the ball between two opposing players at the center of the field. To score, the ball must be kicked last by an active player and must go through the goal at or below shoulder height. A goal counts one point. Sideline players may pass to an active teammate, but a sideline kick cannot score a goal.

Regular rules generally prevail, with special attention to the restrictions of no pushing, holding, tripping, or other rough play. Rough play is a foul and causes a point to be awarded to the other team. For an out-of-bounds ball, the team on the side of the field where the ball went out-of-bounds is awarded a free kick near that spot. No score can result from a free kick. Violation of the touch rule also results in a free kick.

Teaching suggestions: A system of rotation in which active players move to the opposite end of the sideline and new players come forth is necessary. More active players can be added when the class is large, and the distance between goals can be increased. After some expertise is acquired, the cones should be moved in to narrow the goal area. If the ball goes over the end line but not through the goal area, the ball is put into play by a defender with a kick.

Line Soccer

Supplies: A soccer ball, four cones, pinnies
Skills: Most soccer skills, competitive play

Two goal lines are drawn 80 to 120 ft apart. A restraining line is drawn 15 ft in front of and parallel to each goal line. Field width can vary from 50 to 80 ft. Each team stands on one goal line, which it defends. The referee stands in the center of the field and holds a ball. At the whistle, three players (more if the teams are large) run from the right side of each line to the center of the field and become active players. The referee drops the ball to the ground, and the players try to kick it through the other team defending the goal line. The players in the field may advance by kicking only.

A score is made when an active player kicks the ball through the opposing team and over the end line (provided that the kick was made from outside the restraining line). Cones should be put on field corners to define the goal line. A system of player rotation should be set up.

Line players act as goalies and are permitted to catch the ball. Once caught, however, the ball must be laid down immediately and either rolled or kicked. It cannot be punted or drop-kicked.

One point is scored when the ball is kicked over the opponent's goal line below shoulder level. One point is also scored in case of a personal foul involving pushing, kicking, tripping, and the like.

For illegal touching by the active players, a direct free kick from a point 12 yd in front of the penalized team's goal line is given. All active players on the defending team must stand to one side until the ball is kicked. Only goalies defend.

A time limit of 2 minutes is set for any group of active players. If no goal is scored during this time, play is halted and the players are changed.

An out-of-bounds ball is awarded to the opponents of the team last touching it. The regular soccer throw-in from out-of-bounds should be used. If the ball goes over the shoulders of the defenders at the end line, any end-line player may retrieve the ball and put it into play with a throw or kick.

Teaching Suggestion: Line Soccer should be played with the regular soccer rules when possible.
Variations:

1. If there is enough space, the teams can count off by threes. They need not keep any particular order at the end lines but simply come out as active players when their number is called. By using numbers, the teacher can pit different groups against each other.

2. Instead of giving a score for a personal foul, a penalty kick can be awarded. The ball is kicked from 12 yd out, and only three defenders are permitted on the line.

Mini-Soccer

Supplies: A soccer ball, pinnies or colors to mark teams, four cones for the corners
Skills: All soccer skills

Each end of the field has a 21-ft-wide goal marked by jumping standards. A 12-yd semicircle on each end outlines the penalty area. The center of the semicircle is at the center of the goal.

The game follows the general rules of soccer, with one goalie for each side. One new feature, the corner kick, needs to be introduced. This kick is used when the ball, last touched by the defense, goes over the end line but not through the goal. The ball is taken to the nearest corner for a direct free kick, and a goal can be scored from the kick. In a similar situation, if the attacking team last touched the ball, the goalkeeper kick is awarded. The goalie puts the ball down and placekicks it forward.

The players are designated as center forward, outside right, outside left, right halfback, left halfback, fullback, and goalie. Players should rotate positions. The forwards play in the front half of the field, and the guards in the back half. Neither position, however, is restricted to these areas entirely, and all may cross the centerline without penalty.

A foul by the defense within its penalty area (semicircle) results in a penalty kick, taken from a point 12 yd distant, directly in front of the goal. Only the goalie is allowed to defend. The ball is in play, with others waiting outside the penalty area.

Teaching suggestion: Position play should be emphasized. The lines of three should be encouraged to spread out and hold reasonable position.

Variation: The number of players can vary, with some games using as few as three on a side in a more restricted area. If teams have more than seven players, the seven-player game should be maintained but with frequent substitutions.

Lesson Plans for Grades 5-6 - Week 3
Soccer Skills (Lesson 2)

Objectives:
To strike a soccer ball with a variety of body parts
To dribble a ball with the feet
To trap a ball with a variety of body parts
To play a soccer lead-up activity and understand the joy of participation

Equipment Required:
One 8" foam rubber ball or junior soccer ball per student
Cones for marking playing areas
Pinnies for lead-up games
Cones for marking the drill areas and goals

Instructional Activities	Teaching Hints

Introductory Activity -- Move and Freeze

1. Review the run, walk, hop, jump, leap, slide, gallop and skip with proper stopping.
2. Practice moving and stopping correctly—emphasize basics of proper movement.

Add variety by asking students to respond to the some of the following movement factors such as high, low, zigzag, large, small, square, triangles, circles.

Fitness Development Activity -- Teacher Leader Exercises

Encourage youngsters to do the best they can within the specified time limit.

Sitting Stretch	35 seconds
Push-Up Challenges	35 seconds
Power Jumper	35 seconds
Jumping Jacks	35 seconds
Sit-Up Challenges	35 seconds
Single-Leg Crab Kick	35 seconds
Knee to Chest Curl	35 seconds
Windmill	35 seconds
Trunk Twister	35 seconds

Conclude the routine with 2-4 minutes of jogging, walking or other aerobic activity.

See text, p. 163-167 for descriptions of challenges.

See text, p. 174-186 for descriptions of exercises.

Tape alternating segments of silence (10 seconds) to signal a change of exercise and music to signal the duration of exercise (35 seconds).

Increase the duration of exercises by 10% over the previous week.

Lesson Focus -- Soccer Skills (2)

Skills
Divide the skills into four stations and place necessary equipment at each station. Students should practice skills they learned in last week's lesson.
1. Review and practice the long pass. Set up a station with plenty of room and students with a partner. They long pass back and forth to each other.
2. Review the inside-of-the foot pass and trapping: Work with a partner and practice passing and trapping.
3. Practice dribbling skills: Give each student a ball and have them practice dribbling. Move the ball with a series of taps. Start slowly and keep the ball in front of the body.
4. Goalkeeping and shooting: Students work with a partner. One dribbles the ball a short distance and then takes shot at goal. The other partner tries to prevent the score.

Make signs that tell students the skills they are to practice at each station. Set the signs on cones in the areas where students are to practice. Ask students to read the signs before they begin.

The foam training balls are best for teaching introductory soccer skills. They don't hurt students when kicked or when they are struck by a ball.

Drills Using Four or More Players
Use the following partner drills to practice the skills above. Drills for four or more players should be organized so that a rotation gives all players an equal opportunity to practice skills.
1. Shooting. For two-way goal practice, two to six players are divided, half on each side of the goal. The width of the goal can vary, depending on the skill of the players. Two types of shooting should be practiced: (a) kicking a stationary ball from 10 to 20 yards out and (b) preceding a kick with a dribble. In the second type, a restraining line 12 to 15 yards out is needed. This line can be marked by cones.

Using cones or chalk, a grid system of 10-yard squares can be marked on a playing field. The grid can be useful when organizing drills, activities, and small-sized games. The number of squares needed depends on the size of the class, but at least one square for every three students is recommended.

Use at least four balls for this two-way drill. After a period of kicking, the groups should change sides. Ball chasers are the players at the end of each line.

2. Shooting and goalkeeping. Scoring can also be practiced with a goalkeeper. Practice should be done with a stationary ball from 12 yards out (penalty distance) and with kicks preceded by a dribble. The goalie and the chaser should remain for one complete round and then rotate. Having a second ball to play with saves time because play can continue while the chaser is recovering the previous ball.

3. Kicking and trapping. This is an excellent squad drill. Approximately eight players form a circle 15 yards in diameter. Two balls are passed back and forth independently. Passes should be kept low, using primarily the side-of-the-foot kick. Using three balls can be tried also.

4. Passing and shooting. The drill can be done with four to six players. Two balls are needed. A passer is stationed about 15 yards from the goal, and a retriever is behind the goal. The shooters are in line, 20 yards from the goal and to the right. The first shooter passes to the passer, and then runs forward. The passer returns the ball to the shooter. The shooter tries to time her run forward so that she successfully shoots the pass through the goal. Both the passer and the retriever should stay in position for several rounds of shooting and then rotate to become shooters. The first pass can be from a stationary ball. Later, however, the kicker can be allowed to dribble forward a short distance before making the first pass. Reverse the field and practice from the left, shooting with the nondominant leg.

The drills can also be set up as individual stations where students rotate after a specified time.

In soccer drills, two approaches should be recognized. The first is the practice of technique with no opposition from any defense. The second is the skill approach, which involves both offensive and defensive players and perhaps a target. In drills using the skill approach, the goal is to outmaneuver the opponent. Some drills begin with the technique approach and then move to the skill approach.

Game Activity - Soccer Lead-Up Games

Bull's-Eye

Supplies: One soccer ball per player

Skills: Dribbling, protecting the ball

The playing area is a large outlined area--circle, square, or rectangle. One player holds a ball in his hands, which serves as the bull's-eye. The other players dribble within the area. The player with the bull's-eye attempts to throw her ball (basketball push shot) at any other ball. The ball that is hit now becomes the new bull's-eye. The old bull's-eye becomes one of the dribblers. A new bull's-eye cannot hit back immediately at the old bull's-eye. A dribbler should protect the ball with her body. If the group is large, have two bull's-eyes. No score is kept and no one is eliminated.

Line Soccer

See the Lesson Plan, Soccer Skills (Lesson 1) for a complete game description.

Mini-Soccer

See the Lesson Plan, Soccer Skills (Lesson 1) for a complete game description.

Regulation Soccer

Supplies: A soccer ball, pinnies

Skills: All soccer skills

A team usually consists of three forwards, three midfield players, four backline defenders, and one goalkeeper. Forwards are the main line of attack. They need to develop good control, dribbling, and shooting skills, and they must have a strong desire to score. They should be encouraged to shoot frequently. Midfield players tend to be the powerhouse of the team. They need good passing and tackling skills as well as a high level of cardiovascular fitness. Defenders should work well together and know when to tackle. They should play safely by clearing the ball away from their own penalty area, and not risk dribbling or passing toward their own goal unless it is absolutely safe to do so. Goalkeepers must be quick and agile, be good decision makers, and have ball-handling skills.

On the toss of the coin, the winning team gets its choice of kicking off or selecting which goal to defend. The loser exercises the option not selected by the winner.

On the kickoff, the ball must travel forward about 1 yd, and the kicker cannot touch it again until another player has kicked it. The defensive team must be 10 yd away from the kicker. After each score, the team not winning the point gets to kick off. Both teams must be onside at the kickoff. The defensive team must stay onside and out of the center circle until the ball is kicked. Regular soccer rules call for scoring by counting the number of goals made.

Elementary school children usually play 6-minute quarters. There should be a rest period of 1 minute between quarters and 10 minutes between halves.

When the ball goes out-of-bounds on the sideline, it is put into play with a throw-in from the spot where it crossed the line. No goal may be scored, nor may the thrower play the ball a second time until it has been touched by another player. All opponents are to be 10 yd back at the time of the throw.

If the ball is caused to go out-of-bounds on the end line by the attacking team, a goal kick is awarded. The ball is placed in the goal area and kicked beyond the penalty area by a defending player, who may not touch the ball twice in succession. If the ball is touched by a player before it goes out of the penalty area, it is not yet in play and should be kicked again.

If the defensive team causes the ball to go out-of-bounds over the end line, a corner kick is awarded. The ball is placed 1 yd from the corner of the field and kicked into the field of play by an attacking player. The 10-yd restriction also applies to defensive players.

If the ball is touched by two opponents at the same time and caused to go out-of-bounds, a drop ball is called. The referee drops the ball between two opposing players, who cannot kick it until it touches the ground. A drop ball also is called when the ball is trapped among downed players.

If a player is closer to the opponent's goal line than to the ball at a time when the ball is played in a forward direction, it is an offside infraction. Exceptions exist, and a player is not offside when she is in her half of the playing field, when two opponents are nearer their goal line than the attacking player at the moment when the ball is played, or when the ball is received directly from a corner kick, a throw-in, or a goal kick.

Personal fouls involving unnecessary roughness are penalized. Tripping, striking, charging, holding, pushing, and jumping an opponent intentionally are forbidden.

It is a foul for any player, except the goalkeeper, to handle the ball with the hands or arms. The goalkeeper is allowed only four steps and must then get rid of the ball. After the ball has left her possession, the goalkeeper may not pick it up again until another player has touched it. Players are not allowed to screen or obstruct opponents, unless they are in control of the ball.

Penalties are as follows:

1. A direct kick is awarded for all personal fouls and handballs. A goal can be scored from a direct free kick. Examples of infringements are pushing, tripping, kicking a player, and holding.

2. A penalty kick is awarded if direct free-kick infringements are committed by a defender in his own penalty area.

3. An indirect free kick is awarded for offsides, obstruction, dangerous play such as high kicking, a goalkeeper's taking more than four steps or repossessing the ball before another player has touched it, and playing the ball twice after a dead-ball situation. The ball must be touched by a second player before a goal can be scored. The referee should signal if the kick is indirect by pointing one arm upward vertically.

Teaching suggestions: Players should be encouraged to use the space on the field to the best advantage. When a team is in possession of the ball, players should attempt to find a position from which they can pass either behind the player with the ball to give support, or toward the goal to be in a better position to shoot. When a team is forced into defense, the defenders should get "goalside" of attackers (between the attackers and their own goal) to prevent them from gaining an advantage.

From an early stage, players should be taught to give information to each other during the game, especially when they have possession of the ball. Valuable help can be given by shouting instructions such as "Man on," "You have time," or "Player behind," and also by calling for the ball when in a good position to receive a pass.

Lesson Plans for Grades 5-6 - Week 4
Soccer Skills (3)

Objectives:
To strike a soccer ball with a variety of body parts
To dribble a ball with the feet
To trap a ball with a variety of body parts
To play a soccer lead-up activity and understand the joy of participation

Equipment Required:
One 8" foam rubber ball or junior soccer ball per student
Cones for marking playing areas
Pinnies for lead-up games

Instructional Activities	Teaching Hints

Introductory Activity -- Popcorn

Students pair up with one person on the floor in push-up position and the other standing ready to move. On signal, the standing students move over and under the persons on the floor. The person on the floor changes from a raised to a lowered push-up position each time the partner goes over or under them. On signal, reverse positions.

Students should not touch each other when they are going over and under.

Offer a challenge of seeing how many times they can go over and under.

Fitness Development Activity -- Hexagon Hustle

Tape alternating segments of silence and music to signal duration of exercise. Music segments (25 seconds) indicate moving around the hexagon while intervals of silence (30 seconds) announce flexibility and strength development activities.

Hustle	25 seconds
Push-Up from Knees	30 seconds
Hustle	25 seconds
Bend and Twist (8 counts)	30 seconds
Hustle	25 seconds
Jumping Jacks (4 counts)	30 seconds
Hustle	25 seconds
Curl-Ups (2 counts)	30 seconds
Hustle	25 seconds
Crab Kick (2 counts)	30 seconds
Hustle	25 seconds
Sit and Stretch (8 counts)	30 seconds
Hustle	25 seconds
Power Jumper	30 seconds
Hustle	25 seconds
Squat Thrust (4 counts)	30 seconds

Conclude the Hexagon Hustle with a slow jog or walk.

Outline a large hexagon with six cones. Place signs with locomotor movements on both sides of the cones. Locomotor movements to use are: Jogging, skipping, galloping, hopping, jumping, sliding, leaping, and animal movements. Sport movements such as defensive sliding, running backwards, and running and shooting jump shots can also be used.

See text, p. 174-186 for descriptions of exercises.

During the hustle, faster moving students should pass on the outside of the hexagon.

Change directions at times to keep students spaced out properly.

Lesson Focus -- Soccer Skills

Since this is the third week of soccer, emphasis should be placed on playing regulation soccer. Introduce the following skills and devote the rest of the time to the game of soccer

Skills

1. Punting
Used by the goalkeeper only, the punt can be stationary or can be done on the run. The ball is held in both hands at waist height in front of the body and directly over the kicking leg. For the stationary punt, the kicking foot is forward. A short step is taken with the kicking foot, followed by a full step on the other foot. With the knee bent and the toe extended, the kicking foot swings forward and upward. As contact is made with the ball at the instep, the knee straightens, and additional power is secured from the other leg through a coordinated rising on the toes or a hop.

2. Throw-Ins
The throw-in is the only time the ball can be handled by field players with their hands. The throw-in is guided by rules that must be followed closely or the result is a turnover to the other team. The rules are as follows:

   a. Both hands must be on the ball.
   b. The ball must be released from over the thrower's head.
   c. The thrower must face the field.
   d. The thrower may not step onto the field until the throw is released.
   e. Both feet must remain in contact with the ground until the ball is released.
   f. The thrower cannot play the ball until it has been touched by another player on the field.

The throw-in from out of bounds may be executed from a standing or running position. Beginning players should learn the throw without a running start. The feet often are placed one behind the other, with the rear toe trailing along the ground. Delivery of the ball should be from behind the head, using both arms equally. Release should be from in front of the forehead with arms outstretched. Instructional cues to help students perform correctly are "drag your back foot" and "follow through with both hands pointing toward the target."

Game Activity - Soccer Lead-Up Games

Use the Soccer-Lead-Up games from previous lessons #2 and #3.

Lesson Plans for Grades 5-6 - Week 5
Rhythmic Movement (Lesson 1)

Objectives:
To run, stop, and pivot under control without falling
To move rhythmically in a variety of situations
To participate cooperatively in a game setting

Equipment Required:
Signs and cones for Hexagon Hustle
Tape player and music for Hexagon Hustle and rhythms

Instructional Activities	Teaching Hints

Introductory Activity -- Run, Stop and Pivot

The class runs, stops on signal and pivots. Vary the activity by pivoting on the left foot or the right foot, increasing the circumference, and performing pivots in quick succession. Teach both the stride stop (one foot in front of the other) and the jump stop (with both feet parallel to each other) prior to the pivot.

Emphasize bending the knees and lowering the center of gravity.

Students should continue running after the pivot.

Fitness Development Activity -- Hexagon Hustle

Tape alternating segments of silence and music to signal duration of exercise. Music segments indicate moving around the hexagon while intervals of silence announce flexibility and strength development activities.

Hustle	25 seconds
Push-Up from Knees	30 seconds
Hustle	25 seconds
Bend and Twist (8 counts)	30 seconds
Hustle	25 seconds
Jumping Jacks (4 counts)	30 seconds
Hustle	25 seconds
Curl-Ups (2 counts)	30 seconds
Hustle	25 seconds
Crab Kick (2 counts)	30 seconds
Hustle	25 seconds
Sit and Stretch (8 counts)	30 seconds
Hustle	25 seconds
Power Jumper	30 seconds
Hustle	25 seconds
Squat Thrust (4 counts)	30 seconds

Conclude the Hexagon Hustle with a slow jog or walk.

Outline a large hexagon with six cones. Place signs with locomotor movements on both sides of the cones. Locomotor movements to use are: Jogging, skipping, galloping, hopping, jumping, sliding, leaping, and animal movements. Sport movements such as defensive sliding, running backwards, and running and shooting jump shots can also be used. The signs identify the hustle activity students are to perform as they approach a cone.

See text, p. 174-186 for descriptions of exercises.

During the hustle, faster moving students should pass on the outside of the hexagon. Change directions at times to keep students spaced out properly.

Lesson Focus -- Rhythmic Movement (1)

Make dances easy for students to learn by implementing some of the following techniques:
Rhythms should be taught like other sport skills. Avoid striving for perfection so students know it is acceptable to make mistakes. Teach a variety of dances rather than one or two in depth in case some students find it difficult to master a specific dance.
1. Teach the dances without using partners.
2. Allow youngsters to move in any direction without left-right orientation.
3. Use scattered formation instead of circles.
4. Emphasize strong movements such as clapping and stamping to increase involvement.
5. Play the music at a slower speed when first learning the dance.

When introducing a dance, use the following methodology:
1. Tell about the dance and listen to the music.
2. Clap the beat and learn the verse.
3. Practice the dance steps without the music and with verbal cues.
4. Practice the dance with the music.

Records can be ordered from Wagon Wheel Records, 17191 Corbina Lane #203, Huntington Beach, CA (714) 846-8169.

Comin' Round The Mountain (American)

Record: AR 32

Formation: Triple circle of three abreast facing counterclockwise

Directions:

Measures	Action
1--4	Touch left toe on the floor to the front, then to the side. Step the left foot behind the right so the legs are crossed; step the right foot one step to the right; then close the left foot to the right. The rhythm of steps is slow, slow, fast-fast-fast. (Front, side, back, side, together)
5--8	Touch the right toe on the floor to the front, then to the outside. Step the right foot behind the left so the legs are crossed; step the left foot one step to the left; then close the right foot to the left. (Front, side, back, side, together)
9--16	Repeat measures 1--8.
17--20	Moving forward, take a step-hop on the left foot and one on the right foot followed by four walking steps. (Step, hop, step, hop; Walk, 2, 3, 4)
21--32	Repeat measures 17--20 three additional times.

Jessie Polka (American)

Records: MAC 5001; CM 1160

Formation: Circle, couples facing counterclockwise with inside arms around each other's waist

Directions:

Measures	Part I Action
1	Beginning left, touch the heel in front, then step left in place. (Left heel, together)
2	Touch the right toe behind. Then touch the right toe in place, or swing it forward, keeping the weight on the left foot. (Right toe, touch)
3	Touch the right heel in front, then step right in place. (Right heel, together)
4	Touch the left heel to the left side, sweep the left foot across in front of the right. Keep the weight on the right. (Left heel, crossover)

Measures	Part II Action
5--8	Take four two-steps or polka steps forward in the line of direction. (Step, close, step; Step, close, step; Step, close, step; Step, close, step)

Inside-Out Mixer

Record: Any record with a pronounced beat suitable for walking at a moderate speed

Formation: Triple circle (three children standing side by side), facing counterclockwise, with inside hands joined. A pinney can be worn by the center person for identification.

Directions:

Measures	Action
1--4	Take eight walking steps forward. (Forward, 2, 3, 4, 5, 6, 7, 8)
5--8	Form a small circle and circle left in eight steps back to place. (Circle, 2, 3, 4, 5, 6, 7, 8)
9--12	The center person walks forward under the raised arms opposite, pulling the other two under to turn the circle inside out. (Inside-out, 2, 3, 4, 5, 6, 7, 8)
13--16	The trio circles left in eight steps, returning to place. When almost back to place, drop hands. The center person walks forward counterclockwise, and the other two walk clockwise (the way they are facing) to the nearest trio for a change of partners. (Circle, 2, 3, 4, mix, 6, 7, 8)

Cotton-Eyed Joe (American)

Records: Belco 257; MAV 1045

Formation: Double circle of couples with partner B on the right, holding inside hands and facing counterclockwise. Varsouvienne position can also be used.

Directions:

Measures	Action
1--2	Starting with the left foot, cross the left foot in front of the right foot, kick the left foot forward. (Cross, kick)
3--4	Take one two-step backward. (Left, close, left)
5--6	Cross the right foot in front of the left foot; kick the right foot forward. (Cross, kick)
7--8	Do one two-step backward. (Right, close, right)
9--16	Repeat measures 1--8.
17--32	Perform eight two-steps counterclockwise beginning with the left foot. (Step, close, step; Repeat eight times)

Triplet Stoop

Supplies: Music

Skill: Moving rhythmically

The game is played in groups of three with the three youngsters holding hands and marching abreast, counterclockwise. On signal, the outside player of the three continues marching in the same direction. The middle player of the three stops and stands still. The inside player reverses direction and marches clockwise. When the music stops, the groups of three attempt to reunite at the spot where the middle player stopped. The last three to join hands and stoop are put into the center for the next round.

Pacman

Supplies: Markers in the shape of Pacman

Skills: Fleeing, reaction time

Three students are it and carry the Pacman marker. The remainder of the class is scattered throughout the area, standing on a floor line. Movement can only be made on a line.

Begin the game by placing the three taggers at the corners of the perimeter lines. Play is continuous; a player who is tagged takes the marker and becomes a new tagger. If a player leaves a line to escape being tagged, that player must secure a marker and become an additional tagger.

Lesson Plans for Grades 5-6 - Week 6
Rhythmic Movement (Lesson 2)

Objectives:
To run rhythmically to the beat of a tambourine
To perform sustained fitness activity
To participate in simple folk dances
To understand the social significance of folk dances

Equipment Required:
Cones, signs, and tape for Hexagon Hustle
Cageball and 15 playground balls
Music for rhythmic activities
Pinnies

Instructional Activities	Teaching Hints

Introductory Activity -- European Running

Students move around the area to the beat of a tom-tom or tambourine. The step is a trot with the knees lifted. Emphasize proper spacing and moving rhythmically. Stop on a double beat of the tom-tom.

Have the leader move in different shapes and designs. Have class freeze and see if they can identify the shape or formation.

Fitness Development Activity -- Hexagon Hustle

Tape alternating segments of silence and music to signal duration of exercise. Music segments indicate aerobic activity while intervals of silence announce flexibility and strength development activities.

Hustle	25 seconds
Push-Up from Knees	30 seconds
Hustle	25 seconds
Bend and Twist (8 counts)	30 seconds
Hustle	25 seconds
Jumping Jacks (4 counts)	30 seconds
Hustle	25 seconds
Curl-Ups (2 counts)	30 seconds
Hustle	25 seconds
Crab Kick (2 counts)	30 seconds
Hustle	25 seconds
Sit and Stretch (8 counts)	30 seconds
Hustle	25 seconds
Power Jumper	30 seconds
Hustle	25 seconds
Squat Thrust (4 counts)	30 seconds

Conclude the Hexagon Hustle with a slow jog or walk.

Outline a large hexagon with six cones. Place signs with locomotor movements on both sides of the cones. Locomotor movements to use are:
Jogging, skipping, galloping, hopping, jumping, sliding, leaping, and animal movements. Sport movements such as defensive sliding, running backwards, and running and shooting jump shots can also be used. The signs identify the hustle activity students are to perform as they approach a cone.

See text, p. 174-186 for descriptions of exercises.

During the hustle, faster moving students should pass on the outside of the hexagon. Change directions at times to keep students spaced out properly.

Lesson Focus -- Rhythmic Movement (2)

Make dances easy for students to learn by implementing some of the following techniques:
Rhythms should be taught like other sport skills. Avoid striving for perfection so students know it is acceptable to make mistakes. Teach a variety of dances rather than one or two in depth in case some students find it difficult to master a specific dance.
1. Teach the dances without using partners.
2. Allow youngsters to move in any direction without left-right orientation.
3. Use scattered formation instead of circles.
4. Emphasize strong movements such as clapping and stamping to increase involvement.
5. Play the music at a slower speed when first learning the dance.

When introducing a dance, use the following methodology:
1. Tell about the dance and listen to the music.
2. Clap the beat and learn the verse.
3. Practice the dance steps without the music and with verbal cues.
4. Practice the dance with the music.

Records can be ordered from Wagon Wheel Records, 17191 Corbina Lane #203, Huntington Beach, CA (714) 846-8169.

Hora (Hava Nagila) (Israeli)

Records: WT 10001; MAV 1043; RPT 106
Formation: Single circle, facing center, hands joined. The circle can be partial.
Note: The hora is regarded as the national dance of Israel. It is a simple dance that expresses joy. The traditional hora is done in circle formation, with the arms extended sideward and the hands on the neighbors' shoulders. It is easiest to introduce the dance step individually. Once the step is learned, youngsters can join hands and practice the circle formation counterclockwise or clockwise. The clockwise version is presented here.
Directions:
Measures Action

1--3   Step left on the left foot. Cross the right foot in back of the left, with the weight on the right. Step left on the left foot and hop on it, swinging the right foot forward. Step-hop on the right foot and swing the left foot forward. The same step is repeated over and over. (Side, behind, side, swing; Side, swing)

The circle may move to the right also, in which case the same step is used, but the dancers begin with the right foot.

Limbo Rock

Records: WT 10034; RM 2
Formation: Single circle or scattered
Directions:
Measures Part I Action

1--2   Touch left foot in. Touch left foot out. Three steps in place. (In, out, left, right, left)
3--4   Repeat measures 1 and 2 beginning with opposite foot. (In, out, right, left, right)
5--8   Repeat measures 1--4.
Measures Part II Action
9--10   Swivel toes right, swivel heels right. Repeat and straighten feet. (Swivel, 2, 3, straighten)
11--12 Repeat beats 1 and 2 beginning with swivel toes left.
13--14 Jump in, clap; jump out, clap. (Jump, clap, jump, clap)
15--16 Repeat measures 13 and 14. Variation:

Hot Time in the Old Town Tonight (American)

Record: AR-32
Formation: Single circle facing center or a series of lines facing forward
Directions:
Measures Part I Action
1--4   Starting with the left foot, walk backward four steps ending with the feet together. Move forward ending with the feet together. (Back, 2, 3, 4; Forward, 2, 3, 4)
5--6   Place the left heel forward followed by a step on the left beside the right. Repeat beginning with the right heel. (Heel, together, heel, together)
7--8   Bend the knees; straighten the knees; and follow with two claps. (Down, up, clap, clap)
9--16   Repeat measures 1--8.
Measures Part II Action
17--18 Move sideways left with a two-step followed by a stamp with the right foot alongside the left foot. (Left, close, left, stamp)
19--20 Repeat to the right and end with the weight on the left foot. (Right, close, right, stamp)
21--22 Step sideways on the left and stamp the right foot alongside the left foot. Repeat in the opposite direction. (Left, stamp, right, stamp)
23--24 Take four steps in place. (Left, right, left, right)
25--32 Repeat measures 1--8.

Teton Mountain Stomp (American)

Records: Windsor 4615; CM 1243
Formation: Single circle of partners in closed dance position, partners A facing counterclockwise, partners B facing clockwise
Directions:
Measures Action
1--4   Step to the left toward the center of the circle on the left foot, close right foot to the left, step again to the left on the left foot, stomp right foot beside the left but leave the weight on the left foot. Repeat this action, but start on the right foot and move away from the center. (Side, close; Side, stomp; Side, close; Side, stomp)

15

5--8	Step to the left toward the center on the left foot; stomp the right foot beside the left. Step to the right away from the center on the right foot, and stomp the left foot beside the right. In "banjo" position (modified closed position with right hips adjacent), partner A takes four walking steps forward while partner B takes four steps backward, starting on the right foot. (Side, stomp, side, stomp; Walk, 2, 3, 4)
9--12	Partners change to sidecar position (modified closed position with left hips adjacent) by each making a one half turn to the right in place, A remaining on the inside and B on the outside. A walks backward while B walks four steps forward. Partners change back to banjo position with right hips adjacent by each making a left-face one half turn; then they immediately release from each other. A walks forward four steps to meet the second B approaching, while B walks forward four steps to meet the second A approaching. (Change, 2, 3, 4; New partner, 2, 3, 4)
13--16	New partners join inside hands and do four two-steps forward, beginning with A's right foot and B's left. (Step, close, step; Repeat four times)

Game Activity

Cageball Target Throw

Supplies: A cageball (18- to 30-in.), 12 to 15 smaller balls of various sizes

Skill: Throwing

An area about 20 ft wide is marked across the center of the playing area, with a cageball in the center. The object of the game is to throw the smaller balls against the cageball, thus forcing it across the line in front of the other team. Players may come up to the line to throw, but they may not throw while inside the cageball area. A player may enter the area, however, to recover a ball. No one is to touch the cageball at any time, nor may the cageball be pushed by a ball in the hands of a player.

Teaching suggestion: If the cageball seems to roll too easily, it should be deflated slightly. The throwing balls can be of almost any size--soccer balls, volleyballs, playground balls, or whatever.

Variation: Two rovers, one from each team, can occupy the center area to retrieve balls. These players cannot block throws or prevent a ball from hitting the target. They are there for the sole purpose of retrieving balls for their team.

Chain Tag

Supplies: None

Skills: Running, dodging

Two parallel lines are established about 50 ft apart. The center is occupied by three players who form a chain with joined hands. The players with free hands on either end of the chain do the tagging. All other players line up on one of the parallel lines.

The players in the center call "Come," and children cross from one line to the other. The chain tries to tag the runners. Anyone caught joins the chain. When the chain becomes too long, it should be divided into several smaller chains.

Variation: Catch of Fish. The chain catches children by surrounding them like a fishing net. The runners cannot run under or through the links of the net.

Lesson Plans for Grades 5-6 - Week 7
Racquet Sport Skills

Objectives:
To exercise independently in the circuit training activity
To understand the difference in racquet strokes between sports
To compete in the game of volley tennis

Equipment Required:
Circuit training music and signs; cones
One racquet and ball for each student
Volleyballs for volley tennis

Instructional Activities	Teaching Hints

Introductory Activity -- Hospital Tag

All students are it. When tagged, they must cover that area of their body with one hand. Students may be tagged twice, but they must be able to hold both tagged spots and keep moving. When a student is tagged three times, he must freeze.

Restart the game when the majority of students have been frozen. It is counterproductive to wait until the last student is frozen.

Fitness Development Activity -- Circuit Training

Students do the best they can at each station within the time limit. This implies that not all youngsters are required to do the same workload. Children differ and their ability to perform fitness workloads differs. Make fitness a personal challenge.
Rope Jumping
Triceps Push-Ups
Agility Run
Body Circles
Hula Hoops
Reverse Curls
Crab Walk
Tortoise and Hare
Bend and Twist
Conclude circuit training with 2-4 minutes of walking, jogging, rope jumping or other self-paced aerobic activity

Tape alternating segments of silence and music to signal duration of exercise. Music segments (begin at 30 seconds) indicate activity at each station while intervals of silence (10 seconds) announce it is time to stop and move forward to the next station.

Use signals such as start, stop, and move up to ensure rapid movement to the next station.

See text, p. 174-186 for descriptions of exercises.

Lesson Focus -- Racquet Sport Skills

1. Discuss the proper method of holding the racquet using the forehand and backhand grips.
2. Air dribble the ball and try the following challenges:
   a. How many bounces without touching the floor?
   b. Bounce it as high as possible. Perform a heel click (or other stunt) while the ball is in the air.
   c. Kneel, sit and lie down while air dribbling.
3. Dribble the ball on the floor with the racquet:
   a. Move in different directions—forward, backward, sideways.
   b. Move using different steps, such as skip, grapevine, gallop.
   c. Move to a kneeling, sitting and supine position while continuing the dribble. Return to a standing position.
4. Bounce the ball off the racquet and "catch" it with the racquet.
5. Place the ball on the floor:
   a. Scoop it up with the racquet.
   b. Roll the ball and scoop it up with the racquet.
   c. Start dribbling the ball without touching it with the hands.
6. Self-toss and hit to a fence, net or tumbling mat. This drill should be used to practice the forehand and backhand. The ball should be dropped so it bounces to waist level.
7. Partner activities:
   a. One partner feeds the ball to the other, who returns the ball with a forehand or backhand stroke.
   b. Stroke the ball back and forth to each other with one or more bounces between contact.
   c. Self-toss and hit. Drop the ball and stroke it to a partner 20-30 feet away. Partner does the same thing to return the ball.

The focus of this unit should be to give youngsters an introduction to tennis, badminton and racquetball. Give students two or three activities to practice so you have time to move and help youngsters. Alternate activities from each of the categories so students receive a variety of skills to practice.

Use instructional cues to improve technique:
a. Hold the wrist reasonably stiff.
b. Use a smooth arm action.
c. Stroke through the ball and follow through.
d. Watch the ball strike the paddle.

Proper grip must be emphasized, and seeing that children maintain this is a constant battle. The easiest method to teach the proper grip is to have the student hold the paddle perpendicular to the floor and shake hands with it. Practice in racquet work should move from individual to partner work as quickly as is feasible, because partner work is basic to racquet sports.

d. Partner throw and hit. One partner throws the ball to the other, who returns the ball by stroking it with the racquet.

   e. Wall volley: If a wall is available, partners can volley against it.

8. Serving:

   a. Teach tennis serve without a racquet. Use a yarn ball and practice hitting it with the open hand. The serve is similar to the overhand throwing motion. The toss is a skill that will need to be mastered prior to learning the striking motion.

   b. Teach the racquetball serve in similar fashion. The hard, driving serve is done using a side-underhand throwing motion. The striking hand should be raised on the backswing. A small foam (Nerf) ball that bounces should be dropped to the floor and struck on the rebound.

   c. For a racquetball lob serve, the ball is bounced and hit with an underhand motion. The ball is hit high on the wall and bounces to the back wall.

   d. The foam ball can be used for the badminton serve also. For this serve, the ball is dropped and hit with an underhand motion before it hits the floor.

   e. Depending on facilities, racquets can be used after the basic motion has been learned.

For the forehand stroke, the body is turned sideways; for a right-handed player, the left side points in the direction of the hit.

For the backhand stroke, the thumb is placed against the handle of the racquet for added support and force, and the body is turned sideways so the shoulder on the side of the racquet hand points in the direction of the stroke.

During either type of stroke, a step is made with the foot that is forward with respect to the direction of the stroke.

Game Activity

Volley Tennis

Supplies: A volleyball

Skills: Most volleyball and tennis skills

The game can be played as a combination of volleyball and tennis. The net is put on the ground, as in tennis, and the ball is put into play with a serve. It may bounce once or can be passed directly to a teammate. The ball must be hit three times before going over the net. Spiking is common because of the low net. A point is scored when it cannot be returned over the net to the opposing team.

One-Wall Handball and Racquetball

Supplies: Racquetballs (or tennis balls) and racquets

Skills: Racquet skills

Two players find a wall and volley the ball back and forth off the wall. Rules can be developed by players for the serve style and what constitutes out of bounds. The basic rule is that the ball can only bounce once on its return from the wall. When a player returns the ball to the wall, it cannot touch the floor before it hits the wall. Any of these rules can be modified by agreement of the players.

Lesson Plans for Grades 5-6 - Week 8
Football Skills (Lesson 1)

Objectives:
To participate in tag games in a cooperative fashion
To participate in a balanced fitness routine
To learn the basic rules of football
To perform the basic skills of football
To enjoy participating in football lead-up activities

Equipment Required:
Signs, cones, and tape for circuit training
4-6 individual jump ropes
4 soccer balls or foam rubber balls
12 cones for boundaries
One flag belt for each student

Instructional Activities	Teaching Hints

Introductory Activity -- Medic Tag

Three or four students are designated as "taggers." They try to tag the others; when tagged, a student kneels down as if injured. Another student (not one of the taggers) can "rehabilitate" the injured player, enabling her to reenter play.

Different types of rehabilitation can be used. The easiest is to touch a body part or run a full circle around the person.

Fitness Development Activity -- Circuit Training

Students do the best they can at each station within the time limit. This implies that not all youngsters are required to do the same workload. Children differ and their ability to perform fitness workloads differs. Make fitness a personal challenge.
Rope Jumping
Triceps Push-Ups
Agility Run
Body Circles
Hula Hoops
Reverse Curls
Crab Walk
Tortoise and Hare
Bend and Twist

Conclude circuit training with 2-4 minutes of walking, jogging, rope jumping or other self-paced aerobic activity.

Tape alternating segments of silence and music to signal duration of exercise. Music segments (begin at 30 seconds) indicate activity at each station while intervals of silence (10 seconds) announce it is time to stop and move forward to the next station.

Use signals such as start, stop, and move up to ensure rapid movement to the next station.

See text, p. 174-186 for descriptions of exercises.

Lesson Focus -- Football Skills

Skills
Practice the following skills:
1. Forward Passing
   The ball should be gripped lightly behind the middle with the fingers on the lace. The thumbs and fingers should be relaxed. In throwing, the opposing foot should point in the direction of the pass, with the body turned sideways. In preparation for the pass, the ball is raised up and held over the shoulders. The ball is delivered directly forward with an overhand movement of the arm and with the index finger pointing toward the line of flight.
2. Catching
   When making a catch, the receiver should keep both eyes on the ball and catch it in the hands with a slight give. As soon as the ball is caught, it should be tucked into the carrying position. The little fingers are together for most catches.
3. Centering
   Centering involves transferring the ball, on a signal, to the quarterback. In elementary school, the shotgun formation is most often used. This requires snapping the ball a few yards backward to the quarterback. A direct snap involves placing the hands under the buttocks of the center. The ball is then lifted, rotated a quarter turn, and snapped into the hands of the quarterback.

   The centering player takes a position with the feet well spread and toes pointed straight ahead. Knees are bent and close enough to the ball to reach it with a slight stretch. The right hand takes about the same grip as is used in passing. The other hand is on the side near the back of the ball and merely acts as a guide. On signal from the quarterback, the center extends the arms backward through the legs and centers the ball to the quarterback.

Use instructional cues for throwing:
1. Turn the non-throwing side toward the direction of the throw.
2. Throw the ball with an overhand motion.
3. Step toward the pass receiver.

Instructional cues help improve catching technique:
1. Thumbs together for a high pass (above shoulder level).
2. Thumbs apart for a low pass (below shoulder level).
3. Reach for the ball, give, and bring the ball to the body.

Instructional cues for centering include the following:
1. Reach forward for the ball.
2. Snap the ball with the dominant hand.
3. Guide the ball with the non-dominant hand.

4. Punting

The kicker stands with the kicking foot slightly forward. The fingers are extended in the direction of the center. The eyes should be on the ball from the time it is centered until it is kicked, and the kicker should actually see the foot kick the ball. After receiving the ball, the kicker takes a short step with the kicking foot and then a second step with the other foot. The kicking leg is swung forward and, at impact, the leg is straightened to provide maximum force. The toes are pointed, and the long axis of the ball makes contact on the top of the instep. The leg should follow through well after the kick. Emphasis should be placed on dropping the ball properly. Beginners have a tendency to throw it in the air, making the punt more difficult.

Instructional cues for punting are:
1. Drop the football; don't toss it upward.
2. Keep the eyes focused on the ball.
3. Kick upward and through the ball.
4. Contact the ball on the outer side of the instep.

Signs which describe key points for each skill should be placed on cones at each station. Instructional cues should also be placed on the signs so students can analyze their form and performance.

Drills

Set up stations for skill practice. Rotate students to each station.

Station 1 - Stance Practice

Students work with a partner and practice getting into the proper stance position. When stance form is mastered, partners can practice getting into position and racing to cones five yards away. Offensive players should use a 3-point stance with toes pointed forward and head up. Defensive players usually use a 4-point stance with more weight on hands. Blockers should avoid falling and should stay on their toes and in front of defensive player.

Junior size footballs are best for this age group. Regulation size footballs are unacceptable because youngster's hands are too small and the balls are too heavy.

Station 2 - Centering and Carrying the Ball

Students work in pairs and practice centering to each other. The player receiving the ball tucks the ball in and runs 5 to 10 yards.

The ball should be carried with the arm on the outside and the end of the ball tucked into the notch formed by the elbow and arm. The fingers add support for the carry.

Station 3 - Passing and Receiving with a Partner

Students work in pairs and practice passing and receiving the ball. Place emphasis on proper throwing and catching technique. Begin practice with short passes to a stationary receiver. After success, practice throwing to moving receivers, placing emphasis on leading the receiver with the pass.

Station 4 - Punting

Concentrate on technique rather than distance when teaching punting. Emphasize keeping the head down with the eyes on the ball. Drop the football rather than tossing it upward prior to the kick. Work in groups of three. One player is the punter, one the receiver, and one receives the pass from the punt receiver.

For beginning punters, using a round foam rubber ball will be easier than kicking a football. Foam rubber footballs are the next step before using junior size footballs.

Game Activity

Football End Ball

Supplies: Footballs

Skills: Passing, catching

The court is divided in half by a centerline. End zones are marked 3 ft wide, completely across the court at each end. Players on each team are divided into three groups: forwards, guards, and ends. The object is for a forward to throw successfully to one of the end-zone players. End-zone players take positions in one of the end zones. Their forwards and guards then occupy the half of the court farthest from this end zone. The forwards are near the centerline, and the guards are back near the end zone of their half of the court.

The ball is put into play with a center jump between the two tallest opposing forwards. When a team gets the ball, the forwards try to throw over the heads of the opposing team to an end-zone player. To score, the ball must be caught by an end-zone player with both feet inside the zone. No moving with the ball is permitted by any player. After each score, play is resumed by a jump ball at the centerline.

A penalty results in loss of the ball to the other team. Penalties are assessed for the following.
1. Holding a ball for more than 5 seconds
2. Stepping over the end line or stepping over the centerline into the opponent's territory
3. Pushing or holding another player

In case of an out-of-bounds ball, the ball belongs to the team that did not cause it to go out. The nearest player retrieves the ball at the sideline and returns it to a player of the proper team.

Teaching suggestions: Fast, accurate passing is to be encouraged. Players in the end zones must practice jumping high to catch the ball while still landing with both feet inside the end-zone area. A system of rotation is desirable. Each time a score is made, players on that team can rotate one person.

To outline the end zones, some instructors use folding mats (4 by 7 ft or 4 by 8 ft). Three or four mats forming each end zone make a definite area and eliminate the problem of defensive players (guards) stepping into the end zone.

Five Passes

Supplies: A football, pinnies or other identification

Skills: Passing, catching

Players scatter on the field. The object of the game is for one team to make five consecutive passes to five different players without losing control of the ball. This scores 1 point. The defense may play the ball only and may not make personal contact with opposing players. No player can take more than three steps when in possession of the ball. More than three steps is called traveling, and the ball is awarded to the other team.

The ball is given to the opponents at the nearest out-of-bounds line for traveling, minor contact fouls, after a point has been scored, and for causing the ball to go out-of-bounds. No penalty is assigned when the ball hits the ground. It remains in play, but the five-pass sequence is interrupted and must start again. Jump balls are called when the ball is tied up or when there is a pileup. The official should call out the pass sequence.

Speed Football

Supplies: Football, flag for each player

Skills: Passing, catching, running with ball

The ball can be kicked off or started at the 20-yd line. The object is to move the ball across the opponent's goal by running or passing. If the ball drops to the ground or a player's flag is pulled when carrying the ball, it is a turnover and the ball is set into play at that spot. Interceptions are turnovers and the intercepting team moves on offense. Teams must make at least four complete passes before they are eligible to move across the opponent's goal line. No blocking is allowed.

Variation: Playing more than one game at a time on smaller fields will allow more students to be actively involved in the game. This is also an enjoyable game when played with Frisbees.

Developmental Level III

Kick-Over

Playing area: Football field with a 10-yd end zone

Players: Six to ten on each team

Supplies: A football

Skills: Kicking, catching

Teams are scattered on opposite ends of the field. The object is to punt the ball over the other team's goal line. If the ball is caught in the end zone, no score results. A ball kicked into the end zone and not caught scores a goal. If the ball is kicked beyond the end zone on the fly, a score is made regardless of whether the ball is caught.

Play is started by one team with a punt from a point 20 to 30 ft in front of its own goal line. On a punt, if the ball is not caught, the team must kick from the spot of recovery. If the ball is caught, three long strides are allowed to advance the ball for a kick.

Teaching suggestion: The player kicking next should move quickly to the area from which the ball is to be kicked. Players should be numbered and should kick in rotation. If the players do not kick in rotation, one or two aggressive players will dominate the game.

Variation: Scoring can be made only by a dropkick across the goal line.

Lesson Plans for Grades 5-6 - Week 9
Football Skills (Lesson 2)

Objectives:
To correct basic errors in throwing techniques of others
To learn the basic rules of football
To perform the basic skills of football
To enjoy participating in football lead-up activities

Equipment Required:
Signs, cones, and tape for Circuit Training
4-6 individual jump ropes
8 junior or foam rubber footballs
12 cones for boundaries
One flag belt and one pinnie for each student

Instructional Activities	Teaching Hints

Introductory Activity -- Agility Run

Pick two lines or markers 5 to 10 yards apart. Students run (or use other locomotor movements) back and forth between the lines for a specified time (10, 15, or 20 seconds). Students can add a personal challenge by seeing how many times they can move back and forth within the given time limit.

Students can try this with a partner they pick. They can race each other to the lines and back.

Students can walk when necessary.

Fitness Development Activity -- Circuit Training

Students do the best they can at each station within the time limit. This implies that not all youngsters are required to do the same workload. Children differ and their ability to perform fitness workloads differs. Make fitness a personal challenge.
Rope Jumping
Push-Ups
Agility Run
Lower Leg Stretch
Juggling Scarves
Curl-Ups with Twist
Alternate Leg Extension
Tortoise and Hare
Bear Hug
Conclude circuit training with 2-4 minutes of walking, jogging, rope jumping or other self-paced aerobic activity

Tape alternating segments of silence and music to signal duration of exercise. Music segments (begin at 35 seconds) indicate activity at each station while intervals of silence (10 seconds) announce it is time to stop and move forward to the next station.

Use signals such as start, stop, and move up to ensure rapid movement to the next station.

See text, p. 174-186 for descriptions of exercises.

Lesson Focus -- Football Skills

Since this is the second week of football, emphasis should be placed on playing some of the lead-up football games. Review last week's skills and introduce the new skills. Devote the rest of the time to playing the games.
Skills
Practice the following skills:
Review the skills taught last week:
1. Forward Passing
2. Catching
3. Centering
4. Punting
Introduce new skills:
1. Lateral Passing
   Lateral passing is a simple underhand toss of the ball to a teammate. The ball must be tossed sideward or backward to qualify as a lateral. It should be tossed with an easy motion, and no attempt should be made to make it spiral like a forward pass.
2. Blocking
   In blocking for Flag Football, the blocker must maintain balance and not fall to the knees. The elbows are out and the hands are held near the chest. The block should be more of an obstruction than a takeout and should be set with the shoulder against the opponent's shoulder or upper body. Making contact from the rear in any direction not only is a penalty but also could cause serious injury.

Students can work with a partner and practice the skills they learned last week. A ball for each two players will assure the most practice time.

The lateral pass is used when a ball carrier wants to get rid of the ball before being stopped.

Instructional cues for blocking technique are the following:
1. Keep feet spread and knees bent.
2. Keep head up.
3. Stay in front of the defensive player.
4. Move your feet; stay on the balls of the feet.

Game Activity

Speed Football
See the Lesson Plan, Football Skills (Lesson 1) for a complete game description.

Fourth Down
    Supplies: A football
    Skills: Most football skills, except kicking and blocking
    Every play is a fourth down, which means that the play must score or the team loses the ball. No kicking is permitted, but players may pass at any time from any spot and in any direction. There can be a series of passes on any play, either from behind or beyond the line of scrimmage.
    The teams line up in an offensive football formation. To start the game, the ball is placed into the center of the field, and the team that wins the coin toss has the chance to put the ball into play. The ball is put into play by centering. The back receiving the ball runs or passes to any of his teammates. The one receiving the ball has the same privilege. No blocking is permitted. After each touchdown, the ball is brought to the center of the field, and the team against which the score was made puts the ball into play.
    To down a runner or pass receiver, a two-handed touch above the waist is made. The back first receiving the ball from the center has immunity from tagging, provided that he does not try to run. All defensive players must stay 10 ft away unless he runs. The referee should wait for a reasonable length of time for the back to pass or run. If the ball is still held beyond that time, the referee should call out, "Ten seconds." The back must then throw or run within 10 seconds or be rushed by the defense.
    The defensive players scatter to cover the receivers. They can use a one-on-one defense, with each player covering an offensive player, or a zone defense.
    Since the team with the ball loses possession after each play, the following rules are used to determine where the ball should be placed when the other team takes possession.
    1. If a ball carrier is tagged with two hands above the waist, the ball goes to the other team at that spot.
    2. If an incomplete pass is made from behind the line of scrimmage, the ball is given to the other team at the spot where the ball was put into play.
    3. Should an incomplete pass be made by a player beyond the line of scrimmage, the ball is brought to the spot from which it was thrown.
Teaching suggestion: The team in possession should be encouraged to pass as soon as is practical, because children tire from running around to become free for a pass. The defensive team can score by intercepting a pass. Since passes can be made at any time, on interception the player should look down the field for a pass to a teammate.
    Variation: The game can be called Third Down, with the offensive team having two chances to score.

Flag Football
    Supplies: A football, two flags per player (about 3 in. wide and 24 in. long)
    Skills: All football skills
    The field is divided into three zones by lines marked off at 20-yd intervals. There also should be two end zones, from 5 to 10 yd in width, defining the area behind the goal in which passes may be caught. Flag Football is played with two flags on each player. The flag is a length of cloth that is hung from the side at the waist of each player. To down (stop) a player with the ball, one of the flags must be pulled.
    Flag Football should rarely, if ever, be played with 11 players on a side. This results in a crowded field and leaves little room to maneuver. If six or seven are on a team, four players are required to be on the line of scrimmage. For eight or nine players, five offensive players must be on the line.
    The game consists of two halves. A total of 25 plays makes up each half. All plays count in the 25, except the try for the point after a touchdown and a kickoff out-of-bounds.
    The game is started with a kickoff. The team winning the coin toss has the option of selecting the goal it wishes to defend or choosing to kick or receive. The loser of the toss takes the option not exercised by the first team. The kickoff is from the goal line, and all players on the kicking team must be onside. The kick must cross the first zone line or it does not count as a play. A kick that is kicked out-of-bounds (and is not touched by the receiving team) must be kicked again. A second consecutive kick out-of-bounds gives the ball to the receiving team in the center of the field. The kickoff may not be recovered by the kicking team unless caught and then fumbled by the receivers.
    A team has four downs to move the ball into the next zone or they lose the ball. If the ball is legally advanced into the last zone, then the team has four downs to score. A ball on the line between zones is considered in the more forward zone.
    Time-outs are permitted only for injuries or when called by the officials. Unlimited substitutions are permitted. Each must report to the official.
    The team in possession of the ball usually huddles to make up the play. After any play, the team has 30 seconds to put the ball into play after the referee gives the signal.
    Blocking is done with the arms close to the body. Blocking must be done from the front or side, and blockers must stay on their feet.

A player is down if one of her flags has been pulled. The ball carrier must make an attempt to avoid the defensive player and is not permitted to run over or through the defensive player. The tackler must play the flags and not the ball carrier. Good officiating is needed, because defensive players may attempt to hold or grasp the ball carrier until they are able to remove one of her flags.

All forward passes must be thrown from behind the line of scrimmage. All players on the field are eligible to receive and intercept passes.

All fumbles are dead at the spot of the fumble. The first player who touches the ball on the ground is ruled to have recovered the fumble. When the ball is centered to a back, she must gain definite possession of it before a fumble can be called. She is allowed to pick up a bad pass from the center when she does not have possession of the ball.

All punts must be announced. Neither team can cross the line of scrimmage until the ball is kicked. Kick receivers may run or use a lateral pass. They cannot make a forward pass after receiving a kick.

A pass caught in an end zone scores a touchdown. The player must have control of the ball in the end zone. A ball caught beyond the end zone is out-of-bounds and is considered an incomplete pass.

A touchdown scores 6 points, a completed pass or run after touchdown scores 1 point, and a safety scores 2 points. A point after touchdown is made from a distance of 3 ft from the goal line. One play (pass or run) is allowed for the extra point. Any ball kicked over the goal line is ruled a touchback and is brought out to the 20-yd line to be put into play by the receiving team. A pass intercepted behind the goal line can be a touchback if the player does not run it out, even if she is tagged behind her own goal line.

A penalty of 5 yd is assessed for the following:

1. Being offside
2. Delay of game (too long in huddle)
3. Failure of substitute to report
4. Passing from a spot not behind line of scrimmage (This also results in loss of down.)
5. Stiff-arming by the ball carrier, or not avoiding a defensive player
6. Failure to announce intention to punt
7. Shortening the flag in the belt, or playing without flags in proper position
8. Faking the ball by the center, who must center the pass on the first motion

The following infractions are assessed a 15-yd loss:

1. Holding, illegal tackling
2. Illegal blocking
3. Unsportsmanlike conduct (This also can result in disqualification.)

Teaching suggestions: Specifying 25 plays per half eliminates the need for timing and lessens arguments about a team's taking too much time in the huddle. Using the zone system makes the first-down yardage point definite and eliminates the need for a chain to mark off the 10 yd needed for a first down.

Lesson Plans for Grades 5-6 - Week 10
Walking and Jogging Skills

Objectives:
To develop a personalized warm-up routine
To participate in vigorous activity for an extended period fo time
To demonstrate activities which stretch specified body parts

Equipment Required:
Manipulative equipment for jogging (as needed)
Recreation and individual equipment as desired

Instructional Activities		Teaching Hints

Introductory Activity and Fitness Development Activity - Stretching and Jogging

Combine the introductory and fitness activities during the track and field unit. This workout helps students learn to stretch and warm up for demanding activity such as walking and jogging.

Jog for 1-2 minutes		
Standing Hip Bend	30 seconds	
Sitting Stretch	30 seconds	
Partner Rowing	60 seconds	
Bear Hug (do each leg)	40 seconds	
Side Flex (do each leg)	40 seconds	
Trunk Twister	30 seconds	
Self-paced jogging for 2-3 minutes		

See text, p. 174-186 for descriptions of exercises.

Teaching Hints:
Keep stretching activities smooth and sustained. Stretches can be held for 6 to 10 seconds.

Allow students to lead each other in their warm-up routine. A goal should be for students to develop a personal warm-up routine they can use when they are away from school.

Youngsters should work independently during their warm-up. If they desire, they can work with a friend.

Lesson Focus -- Walking and Jogging Skills

The walking and jogging lesson should be a relaxed lesson with emphasis on developing activity patterns that can be used outside of the school environment. An educational approach to this lesson can teach students that walking and jogging is done without equipment and offers excellent health benefits. It is an activity that can literally be done for a lifetime. The following are suggestions for implementing this unit of instruction:

1. Youngsters should be allowed to find a friend with whom they want to jog or walk. The result is usually a friend of similar ability level. A way to judge correct pace is to be able to talk with a friend without undue stress. If students are too winded to talk, they are probably running too fast. A selected friend will encourage talking and help assure that the experience is positive and within the student's aerobic capacity. *Pace, not race* is the motto.

2. Jogging and walking should be done in any direction so people are unable to keep track of the distance covered. Doing laps on a track is one of the surest ways to discourage less able youngsters. They always finish last and are open to chiding by the rest of the class.

3. Jogging and walking should be done for a specified time rather than a specified distance. All youngsters should not have to run the same distance. This goes against the philosophy of accompanying individual differences and varying aerobic capacities. Running or walking for a set amount of time will allow the less able child to move without fear of ridicule.

4. Teachers should not be concerned about foot action, since the child selects naturally the means that is most comfortable. Arm movement should be easy and natural, with elbows bent. The head and upper body should be held up and back. The eyes look ahead. The general body position in walking and jogging should be erect but relaxed. Jogging on the toes should be avoided.

5. Jogging and walking should not be a competitive, timed activity. Each youngster should move at a self-determined pace. Racing belongs in the track program. Another reason to avoid speed is that racing keeps youngsters from learning to pace themselves. For developing endurance and gaining health benefits, it is more important to move for a longer time at a slower speed than to run at top speed for a shorter distance.

6. It can be motivating for youngsters if they run with a piece of equipment, i.e., beanbag or jump rope. They can play catch with a beanbag or roll a hoop while walking or jogging.

Game Activity - Individual or Recreational Activities

When youngsters are finished walking and jogging, allow them the opportunity to participate in a choice of individual or recreational activities.

Lesson Plans for Grades 5-6 - Week 11
Cross-Country Running/Walking

Objectives:
To participate in cross-country activities as a participating team member
To show respect for peers regardless of individual differences in ability
To develop a personalized warm-up routine that enhances flexibility

Equipment Required:
Recreational and individual equipment as needed
8-12 cones for cross-country "funnel"

Instructional Activities	Teaching Hints

Introductory Activity and Fitness Development Activity - Stretching and Jogging

Combine the introductory and fitness activities during the track and field unit. This workout helps students learn to stretch and warm up for demanding activity such as walking and jogging.

Keep stretching activities smooth and sustained. Stretches can be held for 6 to 10 seconds.

Jog for 1-2 minutes	
Standing Hip Bend	30 seconds
Sitting Stretch	30 seconds
Partner Rowing	60 seconds
Bear Hug (do each leg)	40 seconds
Side Flex (do each leg)	40 seconds
Trunk Twister	30 seconds
Self-paced jogging for 2-3 minutes	

Allow students to lead each other in their warm-up routine. A goal should be for students to develop a personal warm-up routine they can use when they are away from school.

Youngsters should work independently during their warm-up. If they desire, they can work with a friend.

See text, p. 174-186 for descriptions of exercises.

Lesson Focus -- Cross-Country Running/Walking

Cross-country courses can be marked with a chalk line and cones so that runners follow the course as outlined. Checkpoints every 220 yards offer runners a convenient reference point so that they can gauge accurately how far they have run. Three courses of differing lengths and difficulty can be laid out. The beginning course can be 1 mile in length, the intermediate 1.25 mile, and the advanced 1.5 mile. Including sandy or hilly areas in the course increases the challenge. When students run cross country, they can select the course that challenges them appropriately.

The attractiveness of cross-country competition lies in the fact that it is a team activity and all members of the team are crucial to its success. Youngsters should learn how to score a meet. Probably the easiest way to keep team scores is to assign seven (depending on class size) members to each team. Points are assigned to finishers based on their placement in the race. For example, the first-place runner receives 1 point, the tenth-place runner 10 points, and so on. The points for all team members are totaled, and the team with the lowest score is declared the winner.

1. Discuss the sport of cross-country running and how it is scored.
   a. Seven members to a team.
   b. Lowest score wins.
   c. Total points for each team based on places finished in race.

2. Divide the class into equal teams by recording times for all members of the class regardless of whether they walked or ran. Create teams of equal ability by dividing students to that the total elapsed time (for all team members) is equal.

3. Depending on the age of youngsters, as well as their ability, teams can run different length courses. The following lengths are suggested:
   a. Beginning—1 mile
   b. Intermediate—1.25 miles
   c. Advanced—1.5 mile

4. Explain how to "warm down" after each course run.

A funnel made of cones at the finish line prevents tying times. As runners go through the funnel, the meet judges and helpers can hand each one a marker with the place of finish on it. This simplifies scoring at the end of the meet. Each team captain can total the scores and report the result.

Game Activity - Individual or Recreational Activities

When youngsters are finished with cross-country running, allow them the opportunity to participate in a choice of individual or recreational activities.

Lesson Plans for Grades 5-6 - Week 12
Individual Rope Jumping Skills (Lesson 1)

Objectives:
To perform exercises to rhythmic accompaniment
To understand the aerobic benefits of rope jumping
To recognize that learning any skill take repetition and refinement

Equipment Required:
One individual jump rope for each student
Exercise to music tape
Base and volleyball for game

Instructional Activities	Teaching Hints

Introductory Activity -- Partner Over and Under

Students pair up with one person on the floor and the other standing ready to move. On signal, the standing students move over, under and/or around the person on the floor. On signal, reverse positions. Students on the floor can also alternate between positions such as curl, stretch and bridge.

Students should see how many different ways they can accomplish the challenge.

Avoid touching each other when moving.

Fitness Development Activity -- Exercises to Music

Forward Lunges	30 seconds
Alternate Crab Kicks	25 seconds
Windmills	30 seconds
Walk and do Arm Circles	25 seconds
Abdominal Crunchers	30 seconds
Side Flex	25 seconds
Triceps Push-Ups	30 seconds
Two-Step or Gallop	25 seconds
Jumping Jack variations	30 seconds
Aerobic Jumping	25 seconds
Leg Extensions	30 seconds
Push-Ups	25 seconds
Walking to cool down	30 seconds

Select music which has a strong rhythm and easy-to-hear beat. When the music is on students perform aerobic activities (for 30 seconds). When the music is not playing, students perform the strength development and flexibility exercises (25 seconds).

See text, p. 174-186 for descriptions of exercises.

Use scatter formation.

Lesson Focus -- Individual Rope-Jumping Skills (1)

1. Introduce the two basic jump rhythms:
    a.   Slow-time rhythm. In slow time rhythm, the performer jumps the rope and then takes a second jump while the rope is overhead. The jump while the rope is overhead is usually a small, light rebound jump. In slow time, the rope make one full turn for each two jumps.
    b.   Fast time rhythm. In fast time rhythm, the student jumps the rope with every jump. The rope makes one full turn for every jump.

2. Introduce some of the basic step variations. The basic steps can be done in slow or fast time.
    a.   Side Swing. Swing the rope, held with both hands to one side of the body. Switch and swing the rope on the other side of the body.
    b.   Double Side Swing and Jump. Swing the rope once on each side of the body. Follow the second swing with a jump over the rope. The sequence should be swing, swing, jump.
    c.   Alternate-Foot Basic Step. In the Alternate-Foot Basic Step, as the rope passes under the feet, the weight is shifted alternately from one foot to the other, raising the non-support foot in a running position.
    d.   Spread Legs Forward and Backward . For Spread Legs Forward and Backward, start in a stride position (as in the Rocker) with weight equally distributed on both feet. As the rope passes under the feet, jump into the air and reverse the position of the feet.
    e. Straddle Jump. Alternate a regular jump with a straddle jump. The straddle jump is performed with the feet spread to shoulder width.

1. The length of the rope is dependent on the height of the jumper. It should be long enough so that the ends reach to the armpits or slightly higher when the child stands on its center. Grades 5 and 6 need a mixture of 7-, 8-, and 9-foot ropes. Ropes or handles can be color-coded for length.

Two types of ropes are available; the beaded (plastic segment) and the plastic (licorice) rope. The beaded ropes are heavier and seem easier to turn for beginning jumpers. The drawback to the beaded ropes is that they hurt when they hit another student. Also, if the segments are made round, the rope will roll easily on the floor and cause children to fall when they step on it. The plastic licorice ropes are lighter and give less wind resistance. For experienced jumpers more speed and control can be gained with this type of rope. An ideal situation would be to have a set of each type.

f. Cross Legs Sideward. In Cross Legs Sideward, as the rope passes under the feet, spread the legs in a straddle position (sideward) to take the rebound. As the rope passes under the feet on the next turn, jump into the air and cross the feet with the right foot forward. Then repeat with the left foot forward and continue this alternation.

g. Toe-Touch Forward. To do the Toe-Touch Forward, swing the right foot forward as the rope passes under the feet and touch the right toes on the next count. Then alternate, landing on the right foot and touching the left toes forward.

h. Toe-Touch Backward. The Toe-Touch Backward is similar to the Swing-Step Sideward, except that the toes of the free foot touch to the back at the end of the swing.

i. Shuffle Step. The Shuffle Step involves pushing off with the right foot and sidestepping to the left as the rope passes under the feet. Land with the weight on the left foot and touch the right toes beside the left heel. Repeat the step in the opposite direction.

3. Teach the Crossing Arms Step

Once the basic steps are mastered, crossing the arms while turning the rope provides an interesting variation. Crossing the arms during forward turning is easier than crossing behind the back during backward turning. During crossing, the hands exchange places. This means that for forward crossing, the elbows are close to each other. This is not possible during backward crossing. Crossing and uncrossing can be done at predetermined points after a stipulated number of turns. Crossing can be accomplished during any of the routines.

4. Teach Double Turning

The double turn of the rope is also interesting. The jumper does a few basic steps in preparation for the double turn. As the rope approaches the feet, the child gives an extremely hard flip of the rope from the wrists, jumps from 6 to 8 inches in height, and allows the rope to pass under the feet twice before landing. The jumper must bend forward at the waist somewhat, which increases the speed of the turn. A substantial challenge for advanced rope jumpers is to see how many consecutive double-turn jumps they can do.

5. Teach shifting from forward to backward jumping

To switch from forward to backward jumping without stopping the rope, any of the following techniques can be used.

a. As the rope starts downward in forward jumping, rather than allowing it to pass under the feet, the performer swings both arms to the left (or right) and makes a half turn of the body in that direction (i.e., facing the rope). On the next downward swing, the jumper spreads the arms and starts turning in the opposite direction. This method also works for shifting from backward to forward jumping.

b. When the rope is directly above the head, the performer extends both arms, causing the rope to hesitate momentarily, at the same time making a half-turn in either direction and continuing to skip with the rope turning in the opposite direction.

c. From a crossed-arm position, as the rope is going above the performer's head, the jumper may uncross the arms and turn simultaneously. This starts the rope turning and the performer jumping in the opposite direction.

6. Teach Jumping with a Partner. One student turns and jumps the rope while her partner enters and jumps simultaneously. The following are some challenges partners can try:

a. Run in and face partner, and both jump.

b. Run in and turn back to partner, and both jump.

c. Decide which steps are to be done; then run in and match steps.

d. Repeat with the rope turning backward.

Posture is an important consideration in rope jumping. The body should be in good alignment, with the head up and the eyes looking straight ahead. The jump is made with the body in an erect position. A slight straightening of the knees provides the lift for the jump, which should be of minimal height (about 1 inch). The wrists supply the force to turn the rope, with the elbows kept close to the body and extended at a 90-degree angle. A pumping action and lifting of the arms is unnecessary. The landing should be made on the balls of the feet, with the knees bent slightly to cushion the shock. Usually, the feet, ankles, and legs are kept together, except when a specific step calls for a different position.

The rope should be held by the index finger and thumb on each side with the hands making a small circle. The elbows should be held near the sides to avoid making large arm circles with the rope.

Music can be added when jumpers have learned the first stages of jumping. Music provides a challenge for continued jumping.

To collect ropes at the completion of a rope-jumping activity, have two or three children act as monitors. They put both arms out to the front or to the side at shoulder level. The other children then drape the ropes over their arms. The monitors return the ropes to the correct storage area.

Instructional cues to use for improving jumping technique are:

a. Keep the arms at the side of the body while turning. (Many children lift the arms to shoulder level trying to move the rope overhead. This makes it impossible for the youngster to jump over the elevated rope.)

b. Turn the rope by making small circles with the wrists.

c. Jump on the balls of the feet.

d. Bend the knees slightly to absorb the force of the jump.

e. Make a small jump over the rope.

7. Teach side by side jumping. Partners clasp inside hands and turn the rope with outside hands.

    a. Face the same direction and turn the rope.

    b. Face opposite directions, clasp left hands, and turn the rope.

    c. Face opposite directions, clasp right hands, and turn the rope.

    d. Repeat routines with inside knees raised.

    e. Repeat routines with elbows locked. Try other arm positions.

Partner jumping may require a slightly longer rope and partners of similar height.

Game Activity

Right Face, Left Face (Maze Tag)

Supplies: None

Skills: Running, dodging

Children stand in rows that are aligned both from front to rear and from side to side. A runner and a chaser are chosen. Children all face the same way and join hands with the players on each side. The chaser tries to tag the runner, who runs between the rows with the restriction that he cannot break through or under the arms. The teacher can help the runner by calling "Right face" or "Left face" at the proper time. On command, the children drop hands, face the new direction, and grasp hands with those who are then on each side, thus making new passages available. When the runner is caught or when children become tired, a new runner and chaser are chosen.

Variations:

    1. Directions (north, south, east, west) can be used instead of the facing commands.

    2. Streets and Alleys. The teacher calls, "Streets," and the children face in one direction. The call "Alleys" causes them to face at right angles.

    3. The command "Air raid" can be given, and children drop to their knees and make themselves into small balls, tucking their heads and seats down.

    4. Having one runner and two chasers speeds up the action.

One Base Tagball

Supplies: A base (or standard), a volleyball (8-in. foam ball for younger children)

Skills: Running, dodging, throwing

A home line is drawn at one end of the playing space. A base or standard is placed about 50 ft in front of the home line. Two teams are formed. One team is scattered around the fielding area, the boundaries of which are determined by the number of children. The other team is lined up in single file behind the home line.

The object of the game is for the fielding team to tag the runners with the ball. Two runners at a time try to round the base and head back for the home line without being tagged. The game is continuous, meaning that as soon as a running team player is tagged or crosses the home line, another player starts immediately.

The fielding team may run with the ball and pass it from player to player, trying to tag one of the runners. The running team scores a point for each player who runs successfully around the base and back to the home line.

At the start of the game, the running team has two players ready at the right side of the home line. The others on the team are in line, waiting for a turn. The teacher throws the ball anywhere in the field, and the first two runners start toward the base. They must run around the base from the right side. After all of the players have run, the teams exchange places. The team scoring the most points wins.

Teaching suggestions: To facilitate tagging a runner, players on the fielding team should make passes to a person close to the runner. They must be alert, because two children at a time are running. The next player on the running team must watch carefully in order to start the instant one of the two preceding runners is back safely behind the line or has been hit.

Lesson Plans for Grades 5-6 - Week 13
Frisbee Skills

Objectives:
To learn the unique throwing style required with frisbees
To learn the rules of frisbee golf
To play a round of frisbee golf in a cooperative manner

Equipment Required:
Cones
Frisbees (one for each pair of students)
Tape for exercise to music
Hoops, bowling pins, and cones

Instructional Activities	Teaching Hints

Introductory Activity -- Move and Manipulate

Each student is given a piece of equipment and moves around the area using locomotor movements. Students toss and catch the equipment while moving. On signal, the equipment is dropped, and students move over and around equipment.

Use any type of equipment available. The goal is to move and be able to manipulate an object.

Fitness Development Activity -- Exercises to Music

Forward Lunges	30 seconds
Alternate Crab Kicks	25 seconds
Windmills	30 seconds
Walk, do Arm Circles	25 seconds
Abdominal Crunchers	30 seconds
Side Flex	25 seconds
Triceps Push-Ups	30 seconds
Two-Step or Gallop	25 seconds
Jumping Jack variations	30 seconds
Aerobic Jumping	25 seconds
Leg Extensions	30 seconds
Push-Ups	25 seconds
Walking to cool down	30 seconds

Select music which has a strong rhythm and easy-to-hear beat. When the music is on students perform aerobic activities (for 30 seconds). When the music is not playing, students perform the strength development and flexibility exercises (25 seconds).

See text, p. 174-186 for descriptions of exercises.

Use scatter formation.

Lesson Focus -- Frisbee Skills

Throwing the Disk
Backhand Throw

The backhand grip is used most often. The thumb is on top of the disk, the index finger along the rim, and the other fingers underneath. To throw the Frisbee with the right hand, stand in a sideways position with the right foot toward the target. Step toward the target and throw the Frisbee in a sideways motion across the body, snapping the wrist and trying to keep the disk flat on release.

Underhand Throw

The underhand throw uses the same grip as in the backhand throw, but the thrower faces the target and holds the disk at the side of the body. Step forward with the leg opposite the throwing arm while bringing the Frisbee forward. When the throwing arm is out in the front of the body, release the Frisbee. The trick to this throw is learning to release the disk so that it is parallel to the ground.

Catching the Disk
Thumb-Down Catch

The thumb-down catch is used for catching when the disk is received at waist level or above. The thumb is pointing toward the ground. The Frisbee should be tracked from the thrower's hand. This clues the catcher about any tilt on the disk that may cause it to curve.

Thumb-Up Catch

The thumb-up catch is used when the Frisbee is received below waist level. The thumb points up, and the fingers are spread.

Throwing and Catching Activities:
a. Throw the Frisbee at different levels to partner.
b. Throw a curve--to the left, right and upward. Vary the speed of the curve.
c. Throw a bounce pass--try a low and a high pass.
d. Throw the disc like a boomerang. Must throw at a steep angle into the wind.
e. Throw the Frisbee into the air, run and catch. Increase the distance of the throw.

Use the following instructional cues to improve skill performance:

a. Release the disk parallel to the ground. If it is tilted, a curved throw results.

b. Step toward the target and follow through on release of the disk.

c. Snap open the wrist and make the Frisbee spin.

If space is limited, all Frisbees should be thrown in the same direction. Students can line up on either side of the area and throw across to each other.

Most activities are best practiced by pairs of students using one disk.

Youngsters can develop both sides of the body by learning to throw and catch the disk with either hand.

f. Throw the Frisbee through a hoop held by a partner.
g. Catch the Frisbee under your leg. Catch it behind your back.
h. Throw the Frisbees into hoops that are placed on the ground as targets. Different-colored hoops can be given different values. Throw through your partner's legs.
i. Frisbee bowling--One partner has a bowling pin which the other partner attempts to knock down by throwing the Frisbee.
j. Play catch while moving. Lead your partner so he doesn't have to break stride.
k. See how many successful throws and catches you can make in 30 seconds.
l. Frisbee Baseball Pitching--Attempt to throw the Frisbee into your partner's "Strike Zone."

Since a Frisbee is somewhat different from the other implements that children usually throw, devote some time to teaching form and style in throwing and catching. Avoid drills that reward speed in throwing and catching.

Game Activity

Frisbee Keep Away
   Supplies: Frisbees
   Skills: Throwing and catching Frisbees
   Students break into groups of three. Two of the players in the group try to keep the other player from touching the Frisbee while they are passing it back and forth. If the Frisbee is touched by the defensive player, the person who through the Frisbee becomes the defensive player. Begin the game by asking students to remain stationary while throwing and catching. Later, challenge can be added by allowing all players in the group move.

Frisbee Golf
   Supplies: One Frisbee per person, hoops for hole markers, cones
   Skills: Frisbee throwing for accuracy
   Frisbee Golf or disk golf is a favorite game of many students. Boundary cones with numbers can be used for tees, and holes can be boxes, hula hoops, trees, tires, garbage cans, or any other available equipment on the school grounds. Draw a course on a map for students and start them at different holes to decrease the time spent waiting to tee off. Regulation golf rules apply. The students can jog between throws for increased activity.
   Disk golf is played like regular golf. One stroke is counted for each time the disk is thrown and when a penalty is incurred. The object is to acquire the lowest score. The following rules dictate play:
   Tee-throws: Tee-throws must be completed within or behind the designated tee area.
   Lie: The lie is the spot on or directly underneath the spot where the previous throw landed.
   Throwing order: The player whose disk is the farthest from the hole throws first. The player with the least number of throws on the previous hole tees off first.
   Fairway throws: Fairway throws must be made with the foot closest to the hole on the lie. A run-up is allowed.
   Dog leg: A dog leg is one or more designated trees or poles in the fairway that must be passed on the outside when approaching the hole. There is a two-stroke penalty for missing a dog leg.
   Putt throw: A putt throw is any throw within 10 ft of the hole. A player may not move past the point of the lie in making the putt throw. Falling or jumping putts are not allowed.
   Unplayable lies: Any disk that comes to rest 6 ft or more above the ground is unplayable. The next throw must be played from a new lie directly underneath the unplayable lie (one-stroke penalty).
   Out-of-bounds: A throw that lands out-of-bounds must be played from the point where the disk went out (one-stroke penalty).
   Course courtesy: Do not throw until the players ahead are out of range.
   Completion of hole: A disk that comes to rest in the hole (box or hoop) or strikes the designated hole (tree or pole) constitutes successful completion of that hole.

Lesson Plans for Grades 5-6 - Week 14
Hockey Skills (1)

Objectives:
To lead other students through warm-up activities
Accept decisions made by game officials in hockey lead-up activities
Identify the benefits of participation in exercises to music

Equipment Required:
Hockey stick and puck for each student
Exercise to music tape
Cones or tumbling mats for goals

Instructional Activities	Teaching Hints

Introductory Activity -- New Leader

Divide class into small groups and appoint one member in each group to lead. Groups move around the area following any movement the leader does. On signal, another person in the group becomes the leader. Various types of locomotor movements and/or exercises can be used by the leader.

Assign each group a specific area if desired. Each area could include a piece of equipment to aid in the activity (beanbag, fleece ball, etc.).

Fitness Development Activity -- Exercises to Music

Side Flex (switch sides)	40 seconds	
Trunk Twister	30 seconds	
Reverse Curls	40 seconds	
Slide/Skip	30 seconds	
Jumping Jack variations	40 seconds	
Triceps Push-Ups	30 seconds	
Abdominal Crunchers	40 seconds	
Gallop	30 seconds	
Push-Ups	40 seconds	
Aerobic Jumping	30 seconds	
Leg Extensions	40 seconds	
Walking to cool down	30 seconds	

Select music which has a strong rhythm and easy-to-hear beat. When the music is on students perform aerobic activities (for 30 seconds). When the music is not playing, students perform the strength development and flexibility exercises (25 seconds).

See text, p. 174-186 for descriptions of exercises.

Use scatter formation.

Lesson Focus -- Hockey Skills (1)

Skills

Practice the following skills:

1. Gripping and carrying the stick.
   The hockey stick should be held with both hands and carried as low to the ground as possible. The basic grip puts the left hand at the top of the stick and the right hand 6 to 12 inches below the left.

   To ensure accuracy as well as safety, the stick must not be swung above waist height.

2. Controlled Dribble.
   The controlled dribble consists of a series of short taps in the direction in which the player chooses to move. The hands should be spread 10 to 14 inches apart to gain greater control of the stick. As the player becomes more skilled, the hands can be moved closer together. The stick is turned so that the blade faces the ball. The grip should not be changed, but rather, the hands should be rotated until the back of the left hand and the palm of the right hand face the ball. The ball can then be tapped just far enough in front of the player to keep it away from the feet but not more than one full stride away from the stick.

   Dribbling instructional cues:
   1. Control the puck. It should always be within reach of the stick.
   2. Hold the stick firmly.
   3. Keep the elbows away from the body.

3. Front Field.
   For the front field, the student must keep an eye on the ball, move to a point in line with its path, and extend the flat side of the blade forward to meet the ball. The faster the ball approaches, the more she must learn to give with the stick to absorb the momentum of the ball. The player should field the ball in front of the body and not permit it to get too close.

   Front fielding instructional cues:
   1. Field with a "soft stick." This means holding the stick with relaxed hands.
   2. Allow the puck to hit the stick and then "give" to make a soft reception.
   3. Keep the hands apart on the stick.

4. Forehand Pass.
   The forehand pass is a short pass that usually occurs from the dribble. It should be taught before driving, because the quick hit requires accuracy rather than distance. The player spreads the feet with toes pointed slightly forward when striking. Approach the ball with the stick held low and bring the stick straight back, in line with the intended direction of the hit. The hands should be the same distance apart as in the carrying position, and the stick should be lifted no higher than waist level. The player's right hand guides the stick down and

   Forehand passing instructional cues:
   1. Approach the puck with the side facing the direction of the pass.

   2. Keep the head down and eyes on the puck.

through the ball. The head should be kept down with the eyes on the ball. A short follow-through occurs after contact.

5. Face-Off

The face-off is used at the start of the game, after a goal, or when the ball is stopped from further play by opposing players. The face-off is taken by two players, each facing a sideline, with their right sides facing the goal that their team is defending. Each player hits the ground on her side of the ball and the opponent's stick over the ball, alternately, three times. After the third hit the ball is played, and each player attempts to control the ball or to pass it to a teammate. The right hand can be moved down the stick to facilitate a quick, powerful movement. An alternate means of starting action is for a referee to drop the ball between the players' sticks.

6. Goalkeeping

The goalie may kick the ball, stop it with any part of the body, or allow it to rebound off the body or hand. He may not, however, hold the ball or throw it toward the other end of the playing area. The goalkeeper is positioned in front of the goal line and moves between the goal posts. When a ball is hit toward the goal, the goalie should attempt to move in front of the ball and to keep his feet together. This allows the body to block the ball should the stick miss it. After the block, the ball is passed immediately to a teammate.

Drills

Use the following drills to practice the skills above:

1. Dribbling
   a. Each student has a stick and ball. On signal, change directions while maintaining control of the ball.
   b. Dribble and dodge imaginary tacklers or dodge around a set of cones. Partners may act as tacklers.
   c. Students in pairs--20 feet apart. One partner dribbles toward the other, goes around him or her, and returns to starting point. The first student then drives the ball to the second, who completes the same sequence.

2. Forehand Passing and Front Fielding
   a. From 8 to 10 feet apart, partners forehand pass and front field the ball back and forth to each other both from moving and stationary positions.
   b. Partners 20 feet apart--players pass the ball back and forth with emphasis on *fielding* and *immediately* hitting the ball back.
   c. The shuttle turn-back formation, in which two files of four or five players face each other, can be used. The first person in the file passes to the first person in the other file, who in turn fields the ball and returns the pass. Each player, when finished, goes to the end of the file.
   d. The downfield drill is useful for polishing passing and fielding skills while moving. Three files of players start at one end of the field. One player from each file proceeds downfield, passing to and fielding from the others until the other end of the field is reached. A goal shot can be made at this point. The players should remain close together for short passes until a high level of skill is reached.

3. Dodging and Tackling Drills
   a. Players are spread out on the field, each with a ball. On command, they dribble left, right, forward, and backward. On the command "Dodge," the players dodge an imaginary tackler. Players should concentrate on ball control and dodging in all directions.
   b. Players work in pairs. One partner dribbles toward the other, who attempts to make a tackle. If the tackle is successful, roles are reversed. This drill should be practiced at moderate speeds in the early stages of skill development.

   c. A three-on-three drill affords practice in many skill areas. Three players are on offense and three are on defense. The offense can concentrate on passing, dribbling, and dodging, while the defense concentrates on tackling. A point is given to the offense when they reach the opposite side of the field. The defensive team becomes the offensive team after a score.

3. Keep the stick below waist level at all times.
4. Drive the stick through the puck.

Hockey is a rough game when children are not taught the proper methods of stick handling. They need to be reminded often to use caution and good judgment when handling hockey sticks.

Ample equipment increases individual practice time and facilitates skill development. A stick and a ball or puck for each child are desirable.

If hockey is played on a gym floor, a plastic puck or yarn ball should be used. If played on a carpeted area or outdoors, a whiffle ball is used. An 8-foot folding mat set on end makes a satisfactory goal.

If hockey is played on a gym floor, a plastic puck or yarn ball should be used. If played on a carpeted area or outdoors, a whiffle ball is used. An 8-foot folding mat set on end makes a satisfactory goal.

Hockey is a team game that is more enjoyable for all when the players pass to open teammates. Excessive control of the ball by one person should be discouraged.

An individual who is restricted to limited activity can be designated as a goalie. This is an opportunity for children with disabilities to participate and receive reinforcement from peers. An asthmatic child, for example, might serve as a goalkeeper.

Fatigue may be a problem. Hockey is a running game that demands agility and endurance. Rotation and rest periods help prevent fatigue.

Lane Hockey

Supplies: Hockey stick per player, puck, two goals

Skills: All hockey skills

The field is divided into eight lanes. A defensive and an offensive player are placed in each of the eight lanes. A goalkeeper for each team is also positioned in front of the goal area. Players may not leave their lane during play. A shot on goal may not be taken until a minimum of two passes have been completed. This rule encourages looking for teammates and passing to someone in a better position before a shot on goal is taken.

Players should be encouraged to maintain their spacing during play. The purpose of the lanes is to force them to play a zone rather than rushing to the puck. A free hit (unguarded) is awarded a team if a foul occurs. Players should be rotated after a goal is scored or at regular time intervals.

Variation: Increase the number of lanes to five or six. This involves a larger number of players. On a large playing area, the lanes may be broken into thirds rather than halves. Increase the number of passes that should be made prior to a shot on goal.

Goalkeeper Hockey

Supplies: One stick per player, a puck or ball

Skills: Passing, fielding, goalkeeping

Each team occupies two adjacent sides of the square. Team members are numbered consecutively from left to right. Two or three numbers are called by the instructor. These players enter the playing area and attempt to capture the ball, which is placed in the center of the square, and to pass it through the opposing team. A point is scored when the ball goes through the opponent's side. Sideline players should concentrate on goalkeeping skills. When a score is made, the active players return to their positions, and new players are called.

Teaching suggestions: The teacher needs to keep track of the numbers called so that all players have an equal opportunity to play. Different combinations can be called.

Sideline Hockey

Supplies: One hockey stick per player, a puck or ball, two 4-by-8-ft folding tumbling mats

Skills: Most hockey skills, except goaltending

Each team is divided into two groups. Half of each team is on the court; these are the active players. The others stand on the sidelines. No goalkeeper is used. A face-off at the center starts the game and puts the ball into play after each score. Each team on the field, aided by the sideline players, attempts to score a goal. The sideline players help keep the ball in bounds and can pass it onto the court to the active players. Sideline players may pass only to an active player and not to each other.

Any out-of-bounds play on a sideline belongs to the team guarding that sideline and is put into play with a pass. An out-of-bounds over the end line that does not score a goal is put into play by the team defending the goal. The group of players on the field change places with the sideline players on their team as soon as a goal is scored or after a specified time period.

Illegal touching, sideline violations, and other minor fouls result in loss of the ball to the opposition. Roughing fouls and illegal striking should result in banishment to the sideline for the remainder of the competitive period.

Teaching suggestions: Some attention must be given to team play and passing strategies rather than having all players simply charge the ball. Teams should use the sideline players by passing to them and receiving passes from them in return. Teams can be rotated so that the same two teams do not face each other continually.

Lesson Plans for Grades 5-6 - Week 15
Hockey Skills (2)

Objectives:
To keep away an object (puck) from opponents in three on three game
To strike a hockey puck so it travels in the desired direction
To understand the basic rules of hockey

Equipment Required:
Hockey stick and puck for each student
Exercise to music tape
Cones or tumbling mats for goals

Instructional Activities	Teaching Hints

Introductory Activity -- Group Over and Under

One half of the class is scattered. Each is in a curled position. The other half of the class leaps or jumps over the down children. On signal reverse the group quickly. In place of a curl, the down children can bridge and the other go under.

The down children can also alternate between curl and bridge, as well as move around the area while in bridge position.

Fitness Development Activity -- Exercises to Music

Side Flex (switch sides)	40 seconds	Select music which has a strong rhythm
Trunk Twister	30 seconds	and easy-to-hear beat. When the music is
Reverse Curls	40 seconds	on students perform aerobic activities
Slide/Skip	30 seconds	(for 30 seconds). When the music is not
Jumping Jack variations	40 seconds	playing, students perform the strength
Triceps Push-Ups	30 seconds	development and flexibility exercises (25
Abdominal Crunchers	40 seconds	seconds).
Gallop	30 seconds	
Push-Ups	40 seconds	See text, p. 174-186 for descriptions of
Aerobic Jumping	30 seconds	exercises.
Leg Extensions	40 seconds	
Walking to cool down	30 seconds	Use scatter formation.

Lesson Focus -- Hockey Skills and Drills (2)

Since this is the final lesson of hockey, devote more time to playing hockey lead-up activities. For specific teaching hints, see the previous lesson (#14).

Skills

Review skills taught in previous lesson:
1. Gripping and carrying the stick.
2. Controlled dribble
3. Front Field
4. Forehand Pass
5. Face-off
6. Goalkeeping

Introduce new skills:

1. Tackling

The tackle is a means of taking the ball away from an opponent. The tackler moves toward the opponent with the stick held low. The tackle is timed so that the blade of the stick is placed against the ball when the ball is off the opponent's stick. The tackler then quickly dribbles or passes in the direction of the goal. Throwing the stick or striking carelessly at the ball should be discouraged. Players need to remember that a successful tackle is not always possible.

2. Dodging

Dodging is a means of evading a tackler and maintaining control of the ball. The player dribbles the ball directly at the opponent. At the last instant, the ball is pushed to one side of the tackler, depending on the direction the player is planning to dodge. If the ball is pushed to the left, the player should move around the right side of the opponent to regain control of the ball, and vice versa. Selecting the proper instant to push the ball is the key to successful dodging. Dodging should not be attempted if a pass would be more effective.

Introduce following drills:
1. Three-on-Three Drill. Set up many goals and allow six students to work in small groups of three offensive and three defensive players.
2. Shooting Drill. Mats are set up as goals (three or four on each end of the floor). Half of class on each half of the floor. Each team attempts to hit pucks into opponents' goals without crossing center line of gym. Use a large number of pucks.

3. Dodging and Tackling Drill. Players work in pairs. One partner dribbles toward the other, who attempts to make a tackle. If the tackle is successful, roles are reversed. This drill should be practiced at moderate speeds in the early stages of skill development.

Game Activity

Sideline Hockey
See Hockey Skills, Lesson 1 (p. 34) for a complete game description.

Regulation Elementary Hockey
Supplies: One stick per player, a puck or ball

Skills: All hockey skills

In a small gymnasium, the walls can serve as the boundaries. In a large gymnasium or on an outdoor field, the playing area should be delineated with traffic cones. The area should be divided in half, with a 12-ft restraining circle centered on the midline. This is where play begins at the start of the periods, after goals, or after foul shots. The official goal is 2 ft high by 6 ft wide, with a restraining area 4 ft by 8 ft around the goal to protect the goalie. Each team has a goalkeeper, who stops shots with her hands, feet, or stick; a center, who is the only player allowed to move full court and who leads offensive play (the center has her stick striped with black tape); two guards, who cannot go beyond the centerline into the offensive area and who are responsible for keeping the puck out of their defensive half of the field; and two forwards, who work with the center on offensive play and who cannot go back over the centerline into the defensive area.

A game consists of three periods of 8 minutes each, with a 3-minute rest between periods. Play is started with a face-off by the centers at midcourt. Other players cannot enter the restraining circle until the ball has been hit by the centers. The clock starts when the puck is put into play and runs continuously until a goal is scored or a foul is called. Substitutions can be made only when the clock is stopped. If the ball goes out-of-bounds, it is put back into play by the team that did not hit it last.

Whenever the ball passes through the goal on the ground, 1 point is scored. If, however, the ball crosses the goal line while in the air, it must strike against the mat or back wall to count for a score. Under no circumstances can a goal be scored on a foul. The puck can deflect off a player or equipment to score, but it cannot be kicked into the goal.

The goalkeeper may use her hands to clear the puck away from the goal, but she may not hold or throw it toward the other end of the playing area. She is charged with a foul for holding the puck. The goalkeeper may be pulled from the goal area but cannot go beyond the centerline. No other player may enter the restraining area without being charged with a foul.

The following are fouls and are penalized by loss of the puck at the spot of the foul.
1. Illegally touching the puck with the hands
2. Swinging the stick above waist height (called sticking)
3. Guards or forwards moving across the centerline
4. Player other than the goalie entering the restraining area
5. Goalie throwing the puck
6. Holding, stepping on, or lying on the puck

Defenders must be 5 yd back when the puck is put into play after a foul. If the spot where the foul occurred is closer than 5 yd to the goal, only the goalkeeper may defend. The puck is then put into play 5 yd directly out from the goal.

Personal fouls include any action or rough play that endangers other players. A player committing a personal foul must retire to the sidelines for 2 minutes. The following are personal fouls.
1. Hacking or striking with a stick
2. Tripping with either the foot or the stick
3. Pushing, blocking

Lesson Plans for Grades 5-6 - Week 16
Basketball Skills (1)

Objectives:
To learn the basic rules of basketball
To participate in a self-directed manner in basketball drills
To work with teammates in basketball lead-up games

Equipment Required:
One basketball or playground ball for
each student
Flags and Pinnies for lead-up games
Cones and tape for exercise routine
Hoops or individual mats for lead-up
games

Instructional Activities	Teaching Hints

Introductory Activity -- Four Corners Sport Movement

Lay out a square with a cone at each corner. Each cone should have a sign on each side listing some type of movement to perform between the cones. Examples are shown in the right hand column. As the students pass each corner, they change to the movement on the sign. On signal, change directions and do the movements on the other side of the sign.

1. Backward Running
2. Long Leaps
3. Carioca
4. Front or Back Crossover Step
5. High Knee/Fast Legs
6. Skipping

Fitness Development Activity -- Astronaut Drills

Walk, do Arm Circles	35 seconds	Tape alternating segments of silence and
Crab Full-Leg Extension	30 seconds	music to signal duration of exercise.
Skip sideways	35 seconds	Music segments indicate aerobic activity
Body Twist	30 seconds	while intervals of silence announce
Slide; change lead leg	35 seconds	flexibility and strength development
Jumping Jack variations	30 seconds	activities.
Crab Walk	35 seconds	
Curl-Ups with Twist	30 seconds	
Hop to center and back	35 seconds	Use scatter formation; ask students to
Four Count Push-Ups	30 seconds	change directions from time to time in
Gallop Backwards	35 seconds	order to keep spacing.
Bear Hugs	30 seconds	
Grapevine Step (Carioca)	35 seconds	See text, p. 174-186 for descriptions of
Trunk Twisters	30 seconds	exercises.
Power Jumper	35 seconds	

Cool down with stretching and walking or jogging for 1-2 minutes.

Lesson Focus -- Basketball Skills, Drills, and Lead-Up Games (1)

Skills

Practice the following skills:

1. Chest (or Two-Hand) Pass

For the chest, or two-hand, pass, one foot is ahead of the other, with the knees flexed slightly. The ball is released at chest level, with the fingers spread on each side of the ball. The elbows remain close to the body, and the ball is released by extending the arms and snapping the wrists as one foot moves toward the receiver.

2. Catching

Receiving the ball is a most important fundamental skill. Many turnovers involve failure to handle a pass properly. The receiver should move toward the pass with the fingers spread and relaxed, reaching for the ball with elbows bent and wrists relaxed. The hands should give as the ball comes in.

3. Dribbling

Dribbling is used to advance the ball, break for a basket, or maneuver out of a difficult situation. The dribbler's knees and trunk should be slightly flexed, with hands and eyes forward. The ball is propelled by the fingertips with the hand cupped and relaxed. There is little arm motion. Students tend to slap at the ball rather than push it. The dribbling hand should be alternated, and practice in changing hands is essential.

Instructional cues help students focus on proper performance of passing.
1. Fingers spread with thumbs behind the ball.
2. Step forward, extend arms, and rotate hands slightly inward.
3. Throw at chest level to the receiver.
4. For bounce passes, bounce the ball past the halfway point nearer the receiver.

Instructional cues for catching include the following:
1. Move into the path of the ball.
2. Spread the fingers and catch with the fingertips.

3. Reach and give with the ball (absorb the force of the ball by reaching and bringing the ball to the chest).

4. Shooting - One-Hand (set) Push Shot

The one-hand push shot is used as a set shot for young children. The ball is held at shoulder-eye level in the supporting hand with the shooting hand slightly below center and behind the ball. As the shot begins, the supporting (nonshooting) hand remains in contact as long as possible. The shooting hand then takes over with fingertip control, and the ball rolls off the center three fingers. The hand and wrist follow through, finishing in a flexed position. Vision is focused on the hoop during the shot. Proper technique should be emphasized rather than accuracy.

Drills

Passing and Catching Drills

1. Slide Circle Drill

In the slide circle drill, a circle of four to six players slides around a person in the center. The center person passes to and receives from the sliding players. After the ball has gone around the circle twice, another player takes the center position.

2. Circle-Star Drill

With only five players, a circle-star drill is particularly effective. Players pass to every other player, and the path of the ball forms a star. The star drill works well as a relay. Any odd number of players will cause the ball to go to all participants, assuring that all receive equal practice.

Dribbling Drills

3. Random Dribbling

Each child has a ball. Dribbling is done in place, varied by using left and right hands. Develop a sequence of body positions (i.e., standing, kneeling, lying on the side, on two feet and one hand). Dribble with each hand.

4. One-Hand Control Drill

Begin with the right hand holding the ball. Make a half circle around the right leg to the back. Bounce the ball between the legs (back to front) and catch it with the right hand and move it around the body again. Change hands.

5. Obstacle, or Figure-Eight, Dribbling

For obstacle, or figure-eight, dribbling, three or more obstacles are positioned about 5 feet apart. The first player at the head of each file dribbles in and around each obstacle, changing hands so that the hand opposite the obstacle is the one always used.

Dribbling and Pivoting Drills

6. File Drill

For the file drill, each player in turn dribbles forward to a designated line, stops, pivots, faces the file, passes back to the next player, and runs to a place at the end of the line. The next player repeats the pattern.

7. Dribble-and-Pivot Drill

For the dribble-and-pivot drill, players are scattered by pairs around the floor. One ball is required for each pair. On the first whistle, the front player of the pair dribbles in any direction and fashion on the court. On the second whistle, she stops and pivots back and forth. On the third whistle, she dribbles back and passes to the partner, who immediately dribbles forward, repeating the routine.

Shooting Drills

8. Basic Shooting Drill

In one simple shooting drill, players form files of no more than four people, and take turns shooting a long and a short shot or some other prescribed series of shots.

9. Set-Shot Drill

In the set-shot drill, players are scattered around a basket in a semicircle, with a leader in charge. Players should be close enough to the basket so that they can shoot accurately. The leader passes to each in turn to take a shot. The leader chases the ball after the shot.

Instructional cues for dribbling include the following:
1. Push the ball to the floor. Don't slap it.
2. Push the ball forward when moving.
3. Eyes forward and head up.

Shooting instructional cues focus on proper form:
1. Keep the shooting elbow near the body.
2. Bend the knees and use the legs.
3. Release the ball off the fingertips.

Baskets should be lowered to 8 or 9 feet, depending on the size of the youngsters.

Lowered baskets help students shoot with proper form. Shooting is not a throw. If students have to throw the ball at the basket, it is too high.

Practice the skills in an individual manner as much as possible. The best alternative is a ball for every student to shoot and dribble. Reduce taking turns as much as possible when practicing skills.

Use junior basketballs or smaller for third and fourth grade students. It is difficult for students to learn skills with regulations size balls. They are too heavy and to large in diameter for youngsters.

Flag Dribble

Supplies: A basketball and a flag for each player

Skill: Dribbling

To play this game, children must have reasonable skill in dribbling. The object is to eliminate the other players while avoiding being eliminated. Players are eliminated if they lose control of the ball, if their flag is pulled, or if they go out-of-bounds. Keeping control of the ball by dribbling is interpreted to mean continuous dribbling without missing a bounce. A double dribble (both hands) is regarded as a loss of control.

The game starts with players scattered around the area near the sidelines. Each has a ball and a flag tucked in the back of her belt. Extra players wait outside the area. On signal, each player begins to dribble in the area. While keeping control of the dribble and staying in bounds, they attempt to pull a flag from any other player's back. They can also knock aside any other player's ball to eliminate that player. As soon as the game is down to one player, that player is declared the winner. Sometimes two players lose control of their basketball at about the same time. In this case, both are eliminated. Sometimes, two players are left and the game results in a stalemate. In this case, both are declared winners and the game starts over.

Variations:

1. If using flags is impractical, the game can be played without this feature. The objective then becomes to knock aside or deflect the other basketballs while retaining control of one's own ball.

2. Flag Dribble can be played by teams or squads. In this case, each squad or team should be clearly marked.

Captain Basketball

Supplies: A basketball, pinnies

Skills: All basketball skills except shooting

A captain's area is laid out by drawing a line between the two foul restraining lines 4 ft out from the end line. The captain must keep one foot in this area. Captain Basketball is closer to the game of basketball than Captain Ball is. The circle restrictions of Captain Ball limit movements of the forwards. Captain Basketball brings in more natural passing and guarding situations, and the game is played in much the same way as basketball.

A team normally is composed of three forwards, one captain, and four guards. The captain must keep one foot in his area under the basket. The game is started with a jump ball, after which the players advance the ball as in basketball. No player may cross the centerline, however. The guards must therefore bring the ball up to the centerline and throw it to one of their forwards. The forwards maneuver and attempt to pass successfully to the captain. A throw by one of the forwards to the captain scores 2 points; a free throw scores 1 point.

Fouls are the same as in basketball. In addition, stepping over the centerline or a guard stepping into the captain's area draws a foul.

In the case of a foul, the ball is given to a forward at the free-throw line. He is unguarded and has 5 seconds to pass successfully to the captain, who is guarded by one player. The ball is in play if the free throw is unsuccessful.

Teaching suggestions: A folding tumbling mat can be used to designate the captain's area at each end of the court. Use of a mat tends to discourage intrusion by guards into the captain's area.

While players are required to remain in their own half of the court, they should be taught to move freely within that area. Short, quick passes should be stressed, because long passes are not effective. This is also good practice for proper guarding techniques.

Sideline Basketball

Supplies: A basketball, pinnies

Skills: All basketball skills

The class is divided into two teams, each lined up along one side of the court, facing the other. The game is played by three or four active players from each team. The remainder of the players, who stand on the sideline, can catch and pass the ball to the active players. Sideline players may not shoot, nor may they enter the playing floor. They must keep one foot completely out-of-bounds at all times.

The active players play regular basketball, except that they may pass and receive the ball from sideline players. The game starts with the active players occupying their own half of the court. The ball is taken out-of-bounds under its own basket by the team that was scored upon. Play continues until one team scores or until a period of time (2 or 3 minutes) elapses. The active players then take places on the left side of their line and three new active players come out from the right. All other players move down three places in the line.

No official out-of-bounds on the sides is called. The players on that side of the floor simply recover the ball and put it into play by a pass to an active player without delay. Out-of-bounds on the ends is the same as in regular basketball. If one of the sideline players enters the court and touches the ball, it is a violation, and the ball is awarded out-of-bounds on the other side to a sideline player of the other team. Free throws are awarded when a player is fouled. Sideline players may not pass to each other but must pass back to an active player. Sideline players should be well spaced along the side.

Lesson Plans for Grades 5-6 - Week 17
Basketball Skills (2)

Objectives:
To learn the basic rules of basketball
To participate in a self-directed manner in basketball drills
To work with teammates in basketball lead-up games

Equipment Required:
One basketball or playground ball for
each student
Pinnies for lead-up games
Cones and tape for exercise routine

Instructional Activities	Teaching Hints

Introductory Activity -- Dribble and Pivot

Students acquire a basketball or playground ball and begin dribbling around the area. On signal, they stop and pivot. On the command "go," they begin dribbling again.

Use both hand while dribbling.

Change the pivot foot every other time.

Fitness Development Activity -- Astronaut Drills

Walk, do Arm Circles	35 seconds	Tape alternating segments of silence and music to signal duration of exercise. Music segments indicate aerobic activity while intervals of silence announce flexibility and strength development activities.
Crab Full-Leg Extension	35 seconds	
Skip sideways	35 seconds	
Body Twist	35 seconds	
Slide; change lead leg	35 seconds	
Jumping Jack variations	35 seconds	
Crab Walk	35 seconds	
Curl-Ups with Twist	35 seconds	See text, p. 174-186 for descriptions of exercises.
Hop to center and back`	35 seconds	
Four Count Push-Ups	35 seconds	
Gallop Backwards	35 seconds	Allow students to adjust the workload pace. They should be allowed to move at a apace that is consistent with their ability level.
Bear Hugs	35 seconds	
Grapevine Step (Carioca)	35 seconds	
Trunk Twisters	35 seconds	
Power Jumper	35 seconds	

Cool down with stretching and walking or jogging for 1-2 minutes.

Lesson Focus -- Basketball Skills, Drills, and Lead-Up Games (2)

Skills
Review previously learned skills (lesson #16) which included: Chest and bounce passes, catching, dribbling and pivoting, and the one-hand set shot.

Introduce new skills:
1. Defending
    Defending involves bending the knees slightly, spreading the feet, and facing the opponent at a distance of about 3 feet. The weight should be distributed evenly on both feet to allow for movement in any direction. Sideward movement is done with a sliding motion. The defender should wave one hand to distract the opponent and to block passes and shots.
2. Lay-Up Shot
    The lay-up is a short shot taken when going in toward the basket either after receiving a pass or at the end of a dribble. In a shot from the right side, the takeoff is with the left foot, and vice versa. The ball is carried with both hands early in the shot and then shifted to one hand for the final push. The ball, guided by the fingertips, should be laid against the backboard with a minimum of spin.
3. Jump Shot
    The jump should be straight up, rather than at a forward or backward angle. The ball should be released at the height of the jump. Since the legs cannot be used to increase the force applied to the ball, the jump shot is difficult for the majority of elementary school youngsters. It may be best to avoid teaching the shot to youngsters who lack enough strength to shoot the ball correctly and resort to throwing it. If the jump shot is presented, the basket should be at the lowest level available and a junior-sized basketball used to develop proper shooting habits.

Instructional cues for proper defending are:
1. Keep the knees bent.
2. Keep the hands up.
3. Don't cross the feet when moving.

Instructional cues for the lay-up shot are:
1. Take off on the foot opposite the shooting hand
2. Lay the ball on the backboard above the basketball.
3. Jump upward and slightly forward on the takeoff.

Another way to practice proper form with the jump shot is to use gray foam balls. They are light and can be shot easily by children. Concentrate on proper form rather than making baskets.

4. Two-Hand Overhead Pass

The two-hand overhead pass is effective against a shorter opponent. The passer is in a short stride position, with the ball held overhead. The momentum of the pass comes from a forceful wrist and finger snap. The pass should take a slightly downward path.

Drills

Review and introduce drills from last week's lesson (#16). Introduce the following new drills:

Jump-Shot Drill

The jump-shot drill is similar to the lay-up drill, except that the incoming shooter receives the ball, stops, and takes a jump shot. The line of shooters should move back so that there is room for forward movement to the shooting spot. As soon as the passer releases the ball to the shooter, he moves to the end of the shooter's line. The shooter goes to the passer's line after shooting

Three Lane Rush Drill

This is a lead-up to the three-player weave, which is difficult for elementary school youngsters to learn. Youngsters are in three lines across one end of the area. The first three players move parallel down the court while passing the ball back and forth to each other. A lay-up shot can be taken as players near the basket.

The jump shot drill may be inappropriate for less strong players. They can choose to shoot the lay-up shot in lieu of the jump shot.

1. Use chest and/or bounce passes.
2. "Lead" the receiver with the pass.
3. Follow your pass, going behind the receiver; then cut for basket, awaiting receipt of a pass.

Game Activity - Basketball Lead-Up Games

Captain Basketball

See Basketball Skills, Lesson 1 (p. 39) for a complete game description.

Sideline Basketball

See Basketball Skills, Lesson 1 (p. 39) for a complete game description.

Twenty-One

Supplies: A basketball

Skills: Shooting

Players are in file formation by teams. Each child is permitted a long shot (from a specified distance) and a follow-up shot. The long shot, if made, counts 2 points and the short shot counts 1 point. The follow-up shot must be made from the spot where the ball was recovered from the first shot. The normal one-two-step rhythm is permitted on the short shot from the place where the ball was recovered.

The first player scoring a total of 21 points is the winner. If the ball misses the backboard and basket altogether on the first shot, the second shot must be taken from the corner.

Variations:

1. A simpler game allows dribbling before the second shot.

2. Players can continue to shoot as long as every shot is made. This means that if he makes both the long and the short shot, a player goes back to the original position for a third shot. All shots made count, and the shooter continues until a miss.

3. The game works well as a team competition, with each player contributing to the team score.

4. Various combinations and types of shots may be used.

Lane Basketball

Supplies: Basketball, pinnies, cones to mark zones

Skills: All basketball skills

The court is divided into six lanes. Players must stay in their lane and cannot cross the midcourt line. Regular basketball rules prevail with the exception that players cannot dribble more than four times. Play is started with a jump ball. At regular intervals, youngsters should rotate to the next lane to assure they get to play all positions.

A number of rule changes can be implemented to change the focus of the game. For example, three passes may be required before shooting may occur. Youngsters could be allowed to move the entire length of the floor within their lane.

One-Goal Basketball

Supplies: A basketball, pinnies (optional)

Skills: All basketball skills

If a gymnasium has four basketball goals, many children can be kept active with this game. If only two goals are available, a system of rotation can be worked out. The game is played by two teams according to the regular rules of basketball but with the following exceptions.

1. The game begins with a jump at the free-throw mark, with the centers facing the sidelines.

2. When a defensive player recovers the ball, either from the backboard or on an interception, the ball must be taken out beyond the foul-line circle before offensive play is started and an attempt at a goal is made.

3. After a basket is made, the ball is taken in the same fashion away from the basket to the center of the floor, where the other team starts offensive play.

4. Regular free-throw shooting can be observed after a foul, or some use can be made of the rule whereby the offended team takes the ball out- of-bounds.

5. If an offensive player is tied up in a jump ball, he loses the ball to the other team.

Fouls are something of a problem, because they are called on individuals by themselves. An official can be used, however.
Variations:

1. A system of rotation can be instituted whereby the team that scores a basket holds the floor and the losing team retires in favor of a waiting team. For more experienced players, a score of 3 or more points can be required to eliminate the opponents.

2. One-on-One. This variation differs from One-Goal Basketball primarily in the number of players. Only two play. Otherwise, the rules are generally the same. The honor system should be stressed since officials usually are not present and players call fouls on themselves. There is more personal contact in this game than in One-Goal Basketball. The game has value because of its backyard recreational possibilities. It is popular because it has been featured on television broadcasts of professional basketball players.

Basketball Snatch Ball

Supplies: Two basketballs, two hoops

Skills: Passing, dribbling, shooting

Each of two teams occupies one side of a basketball floor. The players on each team are numbered consecutively and must stand in the numbered order. The two balls are placed inside two hoops, one on each side of the centerline. When the teacher calls a number, the player from each team whose number was called runs to the ball, dribbles it to the basket on her right, and tries to make the basket. As soon as a successful basket is made, she dribbles back and places the ball on the spot where she picked it up. The first player to return the ball after making a basket scores a point for her team. The teacher should use some system to keep track of the numbers so that all children have a turn. Numbers can be called in any order.

Teaching suggestion: In returning the ball, emphasis should be placed on legal dribbling or passing. In the hurry to get back, illegal traveling sometimes occurs.

Variations:

1. Players can run by pairs, with either a pair of players assigned the same number or the teacher calling two numbers. Three passes must be made before the shot is taken and before the ball is replaced inside the hoop.

2. Three players can run at a time, with the stipulation that the player who picks up the ball from the hoop must be the one who takes the first shot. All players must handle the ball on the way down and on the way back.

3. To make a more challenging spot for the return, use a deck tennis ring. This demands more critical control than placing the ball in a hoop. In either case, the ball must rest within the designated area to score.

4. A more demanding task calls for a single player to pass the ball to each of his teammates successively on the way down and on the way back. Teammates scatter themselves along the sideline after the number has been called.

Lesson Plans for Grades 5-6 - Week 18
Basketball Skills (3)

Objectives:
To learn the basic rules of basketball
To participate in a self-directed manner in basketball drills
To work with teammates in basketball lead-up games

Equipment Required:
One basketball or playground ball for
each student
Pinnies for lead-up games
Cones and tape for exercise routine

Instructional Activities	Teaching Hints

Introductory Activity -- Leapfrog

Two, three or four children are used for this group activity. They form a curved line, with all except the last child in line taking the leapfrog position. The last child leaps over the other children in turn and, after going over the last child, runs 10 steps and gets down in position so that the others can leap him.

Change the height of the leapfrog position—low, medium, high. Increase the distance between the youngsters in the leapfrog position.

Fitness Development Activity -- Astronaut Drills

Walk, do Arm Circles	40 seconds	Tape alternating segments of silence and music to signal duration of exercise. Music segments indicate aerobic activity while intervals of silence announce flexibility and strength development activities.
Crab Full-Leg Extension	35 seconds	
Skip sideways	40 seconds	
Body Twist	35 seconds	
Slide; change lead leg	40 seconds	
Jumping Jack variations	35 seconds	
Crab Walk	40 seconds	
Curl-Ups with Twist	35 seconds	
Hop to center and back	40 seconds	Use scatter formation; ask students to change directions from time to time in order to keep spacing.
Four Count Push-Ups	35 seconds	
Gallop Backwards	40 seconds	
Bear Hugs	35 seconds	
Grapevine Step (Carioca)	40 seconds	Allow students to adjust the workload pace. They should be allowed to move at a apace that is consistent with their ability level.
Trunk Twisters	35 seconds	
Power Jumper	40 seconds	

Cool down with stretching and walking or jogging for 1-2 minutes.

Lesson Focus and Game Activity -- Basketball Skills and Lead-Up Games (3)

Since this is the third week of basketball, emphasis should be placed on playing basketball lead-up games. If necessary, review any skills and drills from the past two weeks of basketball instruction.

Basic Basketball Rules
The game of basketball played at the elementary school level is similar to the official game played in the junior and senior high schools, but is modified to assure the opportunity for success and for proper skill development. A team is made up of five players, including two guards, one center, and two forwards. The game is divided into four quarters, each 6 minutes in length. The game is under the control of a referee and an umpire, both of whom have an equal right to call violations and fouls. They work on opposite sides of the floor and are assisted by a timer and a scorer. The following rules apply to the game for elementary school children.
Putting the Ball into Play
    Each quarter is started with a jump ball at the center circle. Throughout the game, the jump ball is used when the ball is tied up between two players or when it is uncertain which team caused the ball to go out-of-bounds. After each successful basket or free throw, the ball is put into play at the end of the court under the basket by the team against whom the score was made.
Violations
    The penalty for a violation is to award the ball to the opponents near the out-of-bounds point. The following are violations.
1. Traveling, that is, taking more than one step with the ball without passing, dribbling, or shooting (sometimes called walking or steps).
2. Stepping out-of-bounds with the ball or causing the ball to go out-of-bounds.
3. Taking more than 10 seconds to cross the centerline from the back to the front court. (Once in the forward court, the ball may not be returned to the back court by the team in control.)
4. Double dribbling, which is taking a second series of dribbles without another player's having handled the ball; palming (not clearly batting) the ball; or dribbling the ball with both hands at once.

5. Stepping on or over a restraining line during a jump ball or free throw.

6. Kicking the ball intentionally.

7. Remaining more than 3 seconds in the area under the offensive basket, which is bounded by the two sides of the free-throw lane, the free-throw line, and the end of the court.

8. To equalize scoring opportunities, a time limit (30 seconds) may be established during which the offensive team must score or give up the ball.

Fouls

Personal fouls are holding, pushing, hacking (striking), tripping, charging, blocking, and unnecessary roughness. When a foul is called, the person who was fouled receives one free throw. If fouled in the act of shooting and the basket was missed, the child receives two shots. If, despite the foul, the basket was made, the score counts and one free throw is awarded. A player who has five personal fouls is out of the game and must go to the sidelines.

Scoring

basket from the field scores 2 points and a free throw 1 point. In most cases, the 3-point goal is not a consideration due to the distance of the shot. If desired, teachers could create a 3-point line to simulate the game played by older students. The team that is ahead at the end of the game is declared the winner. If the score is tied, an overtime period of 2 minutes is played. If the score is still tied after this period, the next team to score (1 or 2 points) is declared the winner.

Substitutes

Substitutes must report to the official scorer and await a signal from the referee or umpire before entering the game. The scorer will sound the signal at a time when the ball is not in play so that the official on the floor can signal for the player to enter the game.

Sideline Basketball

See Basketball Skills, Lesson 1 (p. 39) for a complete game description.

Flag Dribble

See Basketball Skills, Lesson 1 (p. 39) for a complete game description.

One-Goal Basketball

See Basketball Skills, Lesson 2 (p. 41-42) for a complete game description.

Basketball Snatch Ball

See Basketball Skills, Lesson 2 (p. 42) for a complete game description.

Three-on-Three

Supplies: A basketball

Skills: All basketball skills

An offensive team of three stands just forward of the centerline, facing the basket. The center player has a basketball. Another team of three is on defense and awaits the offensive team in the area near the foul line. The remaining teams, waiting for their turn, stand beyond the end line.

Regular basketball rules are used. At a signal, the offensive team advances to score. A scrimmage is over when the offensive team scores or when the ball is recovered by the defense. In either case, the defensive team moves to the center of the floor and becomes the offensive unit. A waiting team comes out on the floor and gets ready for defense. The old offensive team goes to the rear of the line of waiting players. Each of the teams should keep its own score. Two games can be carried on at the same time, one in each half of the court.

Variations:

1. If the offensive team scores, it remains on the floor, and the defensive team drops off in favor of the next team. If the defense recovers the ball, the offensive team rotates off the floor.

2. If a team has a foul (by one of the players), that team rotates off the floor in favor of the next team.

3. A team wins when it scores 3 points. The contest becomes a regular scrimmage in which the offensive team becomes the defensive team upon recovering the ball. When a team scores 3 points, the other team is rotated off the floor. Rules for One-Goal Basketball prevail.

4. The game can be played with four against four.

Lesson Plans for Grades 5-6 - Week 19
Recreational Activities

Objectives:
To be able to move continuously in moderately active activities
To learn the rules of recreational activities
To play in recreational activities independently without adult supervision

Equipment Required:
Equipment for recreational activities

Instructional Activities	Teaching Hints

Introductory Activity -- Jog and Stretch

The class jogs around the area. On signal, they stop and stretch a body part. Students work independently and are responsible for stretching as many body parts as possible.

Use students to demonstrate a variety of stretches.

Fitness Development Activity -- Aerobic Fitness

The following aerobic movements are suggestions only. When youngsters begin to fatigue, stop the aerobic fitness movements and do some of the flexibility and strength development activities learned in previous lessons. This will allow students time to recover aerobically.

1. Rhythmic run with clap
2. Bounce turn and clap
3. Rhythmic 4-count curl-ups (knees, toes, knees, back)
4. Rhythmic Crab Kicks (slow time)
5. Jumping Jack combination
6. Double knee lifts
7. Lunges (right, left, forward) with single-arm circles (on the side lunges) and double-arms circles (on the forward lunge)
8. Rhythmic trunk twists
9. Directional run (forward, backward, side, turning)
10. Rock side to side with clap
11. Side leg raises (alternate legs)
12. Rhythmic 4-count push-ups (If these are too difficult for students, substitute single-arm circles in the push-up position.)

Use music to stimulate effort. Any combination of movements can be used.

Keep the steps simple and easy to perform. Some students will become frustrated if the learning curve is steep.

Signs which explain the aerobic activities will help students remember performance cues.

Don't stress or expect perfection. Allow students to perform the activities as best they can.

See text, p. 195-199 for description of aerobic activities.

Lesson Focus and Game Activity -- Recreational Activities

The purpose of this unit is to teach children activities that they can play during the time when school is not in session.

1. Shuffleboard
2. Four Square
3. Double Dutch rope jumping
4. Team Handball
5. Around the Key Basketball
6. Beachball Volleyball (2 on 2)
7. Jacks
8. Marbles
9. Sidewalk Tennis
10. Horseshoes
11. Rope Quoits
12. Tetherball
13. Tennis Volleyball

Teach students the rules of recreational activities so they are able to participate effectively during free-time.

Teach any games that are traditional to an area. Older youngsters may be a good source of advice for often-played games.

If desired, set up a number of stations and have youngsters rotate to different stations during the lesson.

Lesson Plans for Grades 5-6 - Week 20
Gymnastics (1)

Objectives:
To understand the principles of stability and balance
To control the body weight in a variety of tumbling and stunt activities
To participate in "one on one" competition and accept the outcome

Equipment Required:
Five hoops and 30 beanbags for Barker's Hoopla
Tumbling mats
Four bowling pins and flags for game activities

Instructional Activities	Teaching Hints

Introductory Activity -- Barker's Hoopla

Place one hoop in each of four corners and in the middle of a square playing area. A distance between hoops of 25-30 feet is challenging. Five or six beanbags are placed in each hoop. There are five teams, one beside each hoop (home base). The object is to take beanbags from other hoops and return them to the home base hoop.

Beanbags must be taken *out* of home base hoop and placed in other hoops. It is not acceptable to pass or throw beanbags. No more than one beanbag may moved at one time.

Fitness Development Activity -- Aerobic Fitness

The following aerobic movements are suggestions only. When youngsters begin to fatigue, stop the aerobic fitness movements and do some of the flexibility and strength development activities learned in previous lessons. This will allow students time to recover aerobically.
1. Rhythmic run with clap
2. Bounce turn and clap
3. Rhythmic 4-count curl-ups (knees, toes, knees, back)
4. Rhythmic Crab Kicks (slow time)
5. Jumping Jack combination
6. Double knee lifts
7. Lunges (right, left, forward) with single-arm circles (on the side lunges) and double-arms circles (on the forward lunge)
8. Rhythmic trunk twists
9. Directional run (forward, backward, side, turning)
10. Rock side to side with clap
11. Side leg raises (alternate legs)
12. Rhythmic 4-count push-ups (If these are too difficult for students, substitute single-arm circles in the push-up position.)

Use music to stimulate effort. Any combination of movements can be used.

Keep the steps simple and easy to perform. Some students will become frustrated if the learning curve is steep.

Signs which explain the aerobic activities will help students remember performance cues.

See text, p. 195-199 for description of aerobic activities.

Alternate bouncing and running movements with flexibility and strength development movements.

Lesson Focus -- Gymnastics Activities (1)

Tumbling and Inverted Balances
Review the Forward Roll

Stand facing forward, with the feet apart. Squat and place the hands on the mat, shoulder width apart, with elbows against the insides of the thighs. Tuck the chin to the chest and make a rounded back. A push-off with the hands and feet provides the force for the roll. Carry the weight on the hands, with the elbows bearing the weight of the thighs. If the elbows are kept against the thighs and the weight is assumed there, the force of the roll is transferred easily to the rounded back. Try to roll forward to the feet. Later, try with the knees together and no weight on the elbows.

Five groups of activities in this lesson ensure that youngsters receive a variety of experiences. Pick a few activities from each group and teach them alternately. For example, teach one or two balance stunts, then a tumbling and inverted balance, followed by a combative, etc. Give equal time to each group of activities

Review the Backward Roll (Handclasp Position)

Clasp the fingers behind the neck, with elbows held out to the sides. From a crouched position, sit down rapidly, bringing the knees to the chest for a tuck to secure momentum. Roll completely over backward, taking much of the weight on the forearms. With this method, the neck is protected.

Scatter tumbling mats throughout the area so that there is little standing in line waiting for a turn.

Forward and Backward Roll Combinations

Begin with a Forward Roll, coming to a standing position with feet crossed. Pivot the body to uncross the feet and to bring the back in the line of direction for a Backward Roll.

Hold the toes, heels, ankles, or a wand while rolling. Use different arm positions, such as out to the sides or folded across the chest. Use a wide straddle position for both the Forward Roll and the Backward Roll.

Balance Stunts

V-Up

Lie on the back, with arms overhead and extended. Keeping the knees straight and the feet pointed, bring the legs and the upper body up at the same time to form a V shape. The entire weight is balanced on the seat. Hold the position for 5 seconds.

Push-Up Variations

Begin the development of Push-Up variations by reviewing proper Push-Up techniques. The only movement is in the arms. The body should come close to, but not touch, the floor. Explore the following variations.

a. Monkey Push-Up. Point the fingers toward each other. Next, bring the hands close enough for the fingertips to touch.

b. Circle-O Push-Up. Form a circle with each thumb and forefinger.

c. Fingertip Push-Up. Get up high on the fingertips.

d. One-Legged Push-Up. Lift one leg from the floor.

Flip-Flop

From a push-up position, propel the body upward with the hands and feet, doing a Turn-Over. Flip back. The stunt should be done on a mat.

Individual Stunts

Wall Walk-Up

From a push-up position with feet against a wall, walk up the wall backward to a handstand position. Walk down again.

Skier's Sit

Assume a sitting position against a wall with the thighs parallel to the floor and the knee joints at right angles. (The position is the same as if sitting in a chair, but, of course, there is no chair.) The hands are placed on the thighs with the feet flat on the floor and the lower legs straight up and down. Try to sit for 30 seconds, 45 seconds, and 1 minute.

Rocking Horse

Lie facedown on a mat with arms extended overhead, palms down. With back arched, rock back and forth.

Heel Click (Side)

Balance on one foot, with the other out to the side. Hop on the supporting foot, click the heels, and return to balance. Try with the other foot.

Partner and Group Stunts

Double Scooter

Two children about the same size face each other, sitting on each other's feet. With arms joined, scoot forward or backward with cooperative movements. When one child moves the seat, the other child should help by lifting with the feet. Progress is made by alternately flexing and extending the knees and hips.

Do not perform many repetitions of tumbling and inverted balances. For most children, limiting the number of forward or backward roll repetitions to four or five will prevent fatigue and injury.

No youngster should be expected to roll over if it is difficult for them. In stunts and tumbling, it is important that the student decide if they are capable and confident enough to try the activity.

Youngsters can do many of the activities around their mats. Many of the activities in this unit do not have to be performed on the mat.

A major concern for safety is the neck and back region. Overweight children are at greater risk and might be allowed to avoid tumbling and inverted balances.

When doing partner stunts and combatives, consider the following instructional procedures:

1. Safety factors must be emphasized. Youngsters should be matched for size; a common method is to ask students to pair up with someone who is similar in height. The length of bouts should be short--- usually 5--10 seconds of contesting is adequate. Children should freeze immediately when the whistle is blown. In tug-of-war contests, no one should let go suddenly to avoid sending other children sprawling backward.

2. Instructions for the contest should be as explicit as necessary. Starting positions should be defined so that both contestants begin in an equal and neutral position. What constitutes a win and the number of trials permitted should be defined.

Tandem Bicycle

One child forms a bicycle position, with back against a wall and knees bent, as if sitting. The feet should be placed under the body. The second child backs up and sits down lightly on the first child's knees. Other children may be added in the same fashion, their hands around the waist of the player immediately in front for support. Forward progress is made by moving the feet on the same side together.

Circle High Jump

tand in circles of three, each circle having children of somewhat equal height. Join hands. One child tries to jump over the opposite pair of joined hands. To be completely successful, each circle must have each child jump forward in turn over the opposite pair of joined hands. (Jumping backward is not recommended.) To reach good height, an upward lift is necessary. Try two small preliminary jumps before exploding into the jump over the joined hands.

Combatives
Hand Wrestle

Starting Position: Contestants place right foot against right foot and grasp right hands in a handshake grip. The left foot is planted firmly to the rear for support.
Action: Try to force the other, by hand and arm pressure, to move either foot. Any movement by either foot means a loss.

Finger Fencing

Starting Position: Contestants stand on the right foot and hold the left foot with the left hand.
Action: Hook index fingers of the right hands and try to push the opponent off balance. Change feet and hands. Any movement of the supporting foot means a loss.

Touch Knees

Starting Position: Contestants stand on both feet and face each other.
Action: Touch one of the opponent's knees without letting the opponent touch yours. Five touches determine the victor.

Grab the Flag

Starting Position: Opponents are on their knees, facing each other on a tumbling mat. Each has a flag tucked in the belt near the middle of the back.
Action: Remain on the knees at all times. Try to grab the flag from the other.

Rooster Fight

Starting Position: Players stoop down and clasp hands behind the knees.
Action: Try to upset the other player or cause the handhold to be released.

3. Fair play should be stressed. Children should be encouraged to find strategies and maneuvers to gain success, but always within the framework of the rules.

4. Contests can be started on signal by the teacher, or children can be allowed to start contests on their own. If children are not self-disciplined, it is best for the instructor to start and stop all contests.

5. To add variety, contests should be done with the right side (arm or leg), the left side, and both sides. Body position can be varied. Children can stand, crouch, sit, or lie for the same contest.

6. Develop a system of rotation, so that youngsters have more than one opponent. Rotating assures that one child will not continually dominate another.

Game Activity

Star Wars

Supplies: Four bowling pins
Skill: Running

A hollow square, about 10 yd on each side, is formed by four teams, each of which occupies one side, facing in. The teams should be even in number, and the members of each team should count off consecutively from right to left. This means that one person on each team has the same number as one child on each of the other three teams. Children are seated cross-legged.

A number is called by the teacher. The four children with the number run to the right, all the way around the square, and through their own vacated space toward the center of the square. Near the center, in front of each team, stands a bowling pin. The first child to put the bowling pin down on the floor is the winner. The pins should be at an equal distance in front of the teams and far enough away from each other to avoid collisions in the center.

Scoring is kept by the words Star Wars. The player who puts the pin down first gets to write two letters of the name. The player who is second gets to write one letter. The lettering can be done in a space in front of each team, where the name would be reasonably protected from the runners. The first team to complete the name is the winner.

Flag Chase

    Supplies: Flags, stopwatch

    Skills: Running, dodging

    One team wears flags positioned in the back of the belt. The flag team scatters throughout the area. On signal, the object is for the chasing team to capture as many flags as possible in a designated amount of time. The flags are brought to the teacher or placed in a box. Players cannot use their hands to ward off a chaser. Roles are reversed. The team pulling the most flags is declared the winner.

Lesson Plans for Grades 5-6 - Week 21
Gymnastics (2)

Objectives:
To understand the principles of stability and balance
To control the body weight in a variety of tumbling and stunt activities
To participate in "one on one" competition and accept the outcome
To play group games and cooperate with teammates

Equipment Required:
Parachute for fitness
Juggling scarves
Tumbling mats
8 to 12 bowling pins and 10 to 15 8"-foam rubber balls

Instructional Activities	Teaching Hints

Introductory Activity -- Following Activity

One partner leads and performs various kinds of movements. The other partner follows and performs the same movements. This can also be done with small groups, with the group following a leader.

Encourage students to challenge their partner. Change partners once or twice to maintain interest in the activity.

Fitness Development Activity -- Parachute Fitness

1. Jog in circle with chute held in left hand. Reverse directions and hold with right hand.
2. Standing, raise the chute overhead, lower to waist, lower to toes, raise to waist, etc.
3. Slide to the right; return slide to the left.
4. Sit and perform curl-ups with a twist.
5. Skip.
6. Freeze, face the center, and stretch the chute tightly with bent arms. Hold for 8-12 seconds. Repeat.
7. Run in place, hold the chute at waist level, and hit the chute with lifted knees.
8. Sit with legs under the chute. Do a seat walk toward the center. Return to the perimeter. Repeat four to six times.
9. Place the chute on the ground. Jog away from the chute and return on signal. Repeat.
10. On sides with legs under the chute. Perform Side Flex and lift chute with legs.
11. Lie on back with legs under the chute. Shake the chute with the feet.
12. Hop to the center of the chute and return. Repeat.
13. Assume the push-up position with the legs aligned away from the center of the chute. Shake the chute with one arm while the other arm supports the body.
14. Sit with feet under the chute. Stretch by touching the toes with the chute. Relax with other stretches while sitting.

Tape alternating segments (25-30 seconds in length) of silence and music to signal duration of exercise. Music segments indicate aerobic activity with the parachute while intervals of silence announce using the chute to enhance flexibility and strength development.

Space youngsters evenly around the chute.

Use different hand grips (palms up, down, mixed).

All movements should be done under control. Some of the faster and stronger students will have to moderate their performance.

Lesson Focus – Gymnastics (2)

Gymnastics
Tumbling and Inverted Balances
Judo Roll

For a left Judo Roll, stand facing the mat with the feet well apart and the left arm extended at shoulder height. Bring the arm down and throw the left shoulder toward the mat in a rolling motion, with the roll made on the shoulder and the upper part of the back. Reverse for a right Judo Roll. Both right and left Judo Rolls should be practiced. Later, a short run and a double-foot takeoff should precede the roll. The Judo Roll is essentially a Forward Roll with the head turned to one side. The point of impact is the back of one shoulder and the finish is a return to the standing position.

Cartwheel

Start with the body in an erect position, arms outspread and legs shoulder width apart. Bend the body to the right and place the right hand on the floor. Follow this, in sequence, by the left hand, the left foot, and the right foot. Perform with a steady rhythm. Each body part should touch the floor at evenly spaced intervals. The body should be straight and extended when in the inverted position. The entire body must be in the same plane throughout the stunt, and the feet must pass directly overhead.

Five groups of activities in this lesson ensure that youngsters receive a variety of experiences. Pick a few activities from each group and teach them alternately. For example, teach an individual stunt or two, then a tumbling skill or inverted balance, followed by a balance stunt, etc. Give equal time to each group of activities

Children who have difficulty with the Cartwheel should be instructed to concentrate on taking the weight of the body on the hands in succession. They need to get the feel of the weight support and later can concentrate on getting the body into proper position.

Cartwheel and Round-Off

Practice the Cartwheel, adding a light run with a skip for a takeoff. To change to a Round-Off, place the hands somewhat closer together during the early Cartwheel action. Bring the feet together and make a quarter turn to land on both feet, with the body facing the starting point. The Round-Off can be followed by a Backward Roll.

Advanced Forward and Backward Roll Combinations

Put together different combinations of Forward Rolls and Backward Rolls. The emphasis should be on choice, exploration, and self-discovery. Variations can involve different approaches, execution acts, and finishes.

Try the following variations of the Forward Roll.

1. Roll while holding the toes, heels, ankles, or a wand.
2. As above, but cross the hands.
3. Roll with hands on the knees or with a ball between the knees.

Try the following suggestions with the Backward Roll.

1. Begin with a Stiff-Legged Sitdown and go into the roll.
2. Roll to a finish on one foot only.
3. Roll with a ball between the knees.

Balance Stunts

Long Reach

Place a beanbag about 3 feet in front of a line. Keeping the toes behind the line, lean forward on one hand and reach out with the other hand to touch the beanbag. Recover in one clean, quick movement to the original position, lifting the supporting hand off the floor. Increase the distance of the bag from the line.

Toe Jump

Hold the left toes with the right hand. Jump the right foot through without losing the grip on the toes. Try with the other foot. (Teachers should not be discouraged if only a few can do this stunt; it is quite difficult.)

Front Seat Support

Sit on the floor, with the legs together and forward. Place the hands flat on the floor, somewhat between the hips and the knees, with fingers pointed forward. Push down so the hips come off the floor, with the weight supported on the hands and heels. Next, lift the heels and support the entire weight of the body on the hands for 3 to 5 seconds. (Someone can help the performer get into position by giving slight support under the heels.)

Individual Stunts

Walk-Through

From a front-leaning rest position, walk the feet through the hands, using tiny steps, until the body is fully extended with the back to the floor. Reverse the body to original position. The hands stay in contact with the floor throughout.

Jump-Through

Starting in a front-leaning rest position, jump the feet through the arms in one motion. Reverse with another jump and return to original position. The hands must push off sharply from the floor, so the body is high enough off the floor to allow the legs to jump under. (Some children may find it easier to swing a little to the side with one leg, going under the lifted hand)

Circular Rope Jump

Crouch down in a three-quarter knee bend, holding a folded jump rope in one hand. Swing the rope under the feet in a circular fashion, jumping it each time. Reverse the direction of the rope. Work from both right and left sides with either a counterclockwise or clockwise turn of the rope.

Bouncer

Start in a push-up position. Bounce up and down with the hands and feet leaving the ground at the same time. Try clapping while doing this. Move in various directions. Turn around.

After practicing Cartwheels, a running approach with a skip can be added before takeoff.

Scatter tumbling mats throughout the area so that there is little standing in line waiting for a turn.

Do not perform many repetitions of tumbling and inverted balances. For most children, limiting the number of forward or backward roll repetitions to four or five will prevent fatigue and injury.

No youngster should be expected to roll over if it is difficult for them. In stunts and tumbling, it is important that the student decide if they are capable and confident enough to try the activity.

Youngsters can do many of the activities around their mats. Many of the activities in this unit do not have to be performed on the mat.

A major concern for safety is the neck and back region. Overweight children are at greater risk and might be allowed to avoid tumbling and inverted balances.

Circular Rope Jump Variations:
1. Perform the rope jump with a partner.
2. Jump using different foot patterns (e.g., one foot or alternate feet) and using slow and fast time.
3. Establish standards for declaring a class champion in different areas. Some categories could be maximum number of turns in 30 seconds, most unique routine, and most jumps without a miss.

Partner and Group Stunts
Two-Way Wheelbarrow

One child holds two wheelbarrows, but with one in front and one behind. The child secures the front wheelbarrow first in a normal wheelbarrow position. The back wheelbarrow assumes position by placing the ankles over the already established hand position of the holder.

Partner Rising Sun

Partners lie facedown on the floor, with heads together and feet in opposite directions. They hold a volleyball or a basketball (or a ball of similar size) between their heads. Working together, they stand up and return to position while retaining control of the ball. Do not touch the ball with the hands.

Partner Rising Sun. A slightly deflated ball works best. Some caution is necessary to prevent bumping heads if the ball is suddenly squeezed out.

Triple Roll

Three children get down on their hands and knees on a mat, with heads all in the same direction to one of the sides. The performers are about 4 feet apart. Each is numbered---1, 2, or 3---with the number 1 child in the center. Number 2 is on the right and number 3 is on the left. Number 1 starts rolling toward and under number 2, who projects upward and over number 2. Number 2 is then in the center and rolls toward number 3, who projects upward and over number 2. Number 3, in the center, rolls toward and under number 1, who, after clearing number 3, is back in the center. Each performer in the center thus rolls toward and under the outside performer.

Triple Roll. Children should be taught that as soon as they roll to the outside, they must get ready to go over the oncoming child from the center. There is no time for delay. The upward projection of the body to allow the rolling child to go under is important.

When doing combatives, consider the following instructional procedures:

Combatives

Palm Push

Starting Position: Contestants face each other, standing 12 inches apart. They place the palms of their hands together and must keep them together throughout the contest.

Action: Try to push the opponent off balance.

Bulldozer

Starting Position: Opponents are on their hands and feet (not knees), facing each other, with right shoulders touching.

Action: Try to push (not bump) each other backward. Pushing across the mat or across a restraining line determines the winner. Change shoulders and repeat.

Breakdown

Starting Position: Opponents are in a front-leaning rest (push-up) position, facing each other.

Action: Using one hand, try to break down the other's position by pushing or dislodging his support while maintaining your own position.

Elbow Wrestle

Starting Position: Contestants lie on the floor or sit at a table and face each other. Their right hands are clasped, with right elbows bent and resting on the surface, and right forearms pressed against each other.

Action: Force the other's arm down while keeping the elbows together. Raising the elbow from the original position is a loss.

Safety factors must be emphasized. Youngsters should be matched for size; a common method is to ask students to pair up with someone who is similar in height. The length of bouts should be short--- usually 5--10 seconds of contesting is adequate. Children should freeze immediately when the whistle is blown.

Instructions for the contest should be as explicit as necessary. Starting positions should be defined so that both contestants begin in an equal and neutral position. What constitutes a win and the number of trials permitted should be defined.

Develop a system of rotation, so that youngsters have more than one opponent. Rotating assures that one child will not continually dominate another.

Game Activity

Team Handball

Supplies: Team handball, foam rubber ball, or volleyball; cones; pinnies
Skills: Running, dribbling, passing, throwing, catching

The object of the game is to move a small soccer ball down the field by passing and dribbling and then to throw the ball into a goal area that is 3 m wide and 2 m high. In regulation play, each team has six court players and one goalie. The six court players cover the entire court. A player is allowed three steps before and after dribbling the ball. There is no limit on the number of dribbles. Dribbling is, however, discouraged because passing is more effective. A double dribble is a violation. A player can hold the ball for 3 seconds only before passing, dribbling, or shooting. Players cannot kick the ball in any way, except the goalie.

One point is awarded for a goal. Violations and penalties are similar to basketball. A free throw is taken from the point of the violation, and defense must remain 3 m away while protecting the goal. A penalty throw is awarded from the 7-m line for a major violation. A major violation occurs when an offensive player who is inside the 9-m line in a good shooting position is fouled. During a penalty throw, all players must be behind the 9-m line.

The offensive team starts the game with a throw-on from the center line. A throw-on also initiates play after each goal. All six offensive players line up at the centerline, and a teammate throws the ball to a teammate. The defense is in position, using either a zone or person-to-person defense. Offensive strategy is similar to basketball with picks, screens, rolls, and movement to open up shots on goal. With a zone defense, short, quick passes are made in an overloaded portion of the zone.

The defensive strategy is similar to basketball, with person-to-person and zone defense being popular. Beginning players should start with the person-to-person defense and learn how to stay with an offensive player. The back players in the zone are back against the goal line, while the front players are just inside the 9-m line. The zone rotates with the ball as passes are made around the court.

Octopus

Supplies: None

Skills: Maneuvering, problem solving

Octopus is a game that gets its name from the many hands joined together in the activity. Children stand shoulder to shoulder in a tight circle. Everyone thrusts the hands forward and reaches through the group of hands to grasp the hands across the circle. Players must make sure that they do not hold both hands of the same player. Players also may not hold the hand of an adjacent player. The object is to untangle the mess created by the joined hands by going under, over, or through fellow players. No one is permitted to release a hand grip during the unraveling. What is the end result? Perhaps one large circle or two smaller connected circles.

Teaching Suggestion: If, after a period of time, the knotted hands do not seem to unravel, call a halt and administer first aid. The teacher and group can decide where the difficulty is and allow a change in position of those hands until the know is dissolved. This should not be used as a competitive game because the difficulty of the knots cannot be equalized.

Bomb the Pins

Supplies: 8 to 12 bowling pins per team, 10 to 12 foam rubber balls

Skill: Throwing

A line is drawn across the center of the floor from wall to wall. This divides the floor into two courts, each of which is occupied by one team. Another line is drawn 25 ft from the centerline in each court. This is the line where each team spaces its bowling pins. Each team has at least five balls.

The object of the game is to knock over the other team's pins--not to throw at opponents. Players throw the balls back and forth, but the players cannot cross the centerline. Whenever a pin is knocked over by a ball or player (accidentally or not), that pin is removed. The team with the most pins standing at the end of the game is declared the winner. Out-of-bounds balls can be recovered but must be thrown from inside the court.

Variations: Pins can be reset instead of removed. Two scorers, one for each pin line, are needed. Rolling the balls is an excellent modification.

Lesson Plans for Grades 5-6 - Week 22
Gymnastics (3)

Objectives:
To understand the principles of stability and balance
To control the body weight in a variety of tumbling and stunt activities
To participate in "one on one" competition and accept the outcome
To play group games and cooperate with teammates

Equipment Required:
Tumbling mats
Parachute and music tape for fitness
12-16 bowling pins

Instructional Activities	Teaching Hints

Introductory Activity -- High Fives

Students move in different directions throughout the area. On signal, they are challenged to run toward a partner, jump, and give a "high five" (slap hands) while moving. Emphasis should be placed on timing so that the "high five" is given at the top of the jump.

Combinations of changing the level of the high five and changing the speed of the locomotor movement can be developed.

Fitness Development Activity -- Parachute Fitness

1. Jog in circle with chute held in left hand. Reverse directions and hold with right hand.
2. Standing, raise the chute overhead, lower to waist, lower to toes, raise to waist, etc.
3. Slide to the right; return slide to the left.
4. Sit and perform curl-ups with a twist.
5. Skip.
6. Freeze, face the center, and stretch the chute tightly with bent arms. Hold for 8-12 seconds. Repeat.
7. Run in place, hold the chute at waist level, and hit the chute with lifted knees.
8. Sit with legs under the chute. Do a seat walk toward the center. Return to the perimeter. Repeat four to six times.
9. Place the chute on the ground. Jog away from the chute and return on signal. Repeat.
10. On sides with legs under the chute. Perform Side Flex and lift chute with legs.
11. Lie on back with legs under the chute. Shake the chute with the feet.
12. Hop to the center of the chute and return. Repeat.
13. Assume the push-up position with the legs aligned away from the center of the chute. Shake the chute with one arm while the other arm supports the body.
14. Sit with feet under the chute. Stretch by touching the toes with the chute. Relax with other stretches while sitting.

Tape alternating segments (25-30 seconds in length) of silence and music to signal duration of exercise. Music segments indicate aerobic activity with the parachute while intervals of silence announce using the chute to enhance flexibility and strength development.

Space youngsters evenly around the chute.

Use different hand grips (palms up, down, mixed).

All movements should be done under control. Some of the faster and stronger students will have to moderate their performance.

Lesson Focus – Gymnastics (3)

Five groups of activities in this lesson ensure that youngsters receive a variety of experiences. Pick a few activities from each group and teach them alternately.

Tumbling and Inverted Balances

Headstand

Begin on a mat in a kneeling position, with hands placed about shoulder width apart and the fingers spread and pointed forward. Place the head forward of the hands, so that the head and hands form a triangle on the mat. Walk the body weight forward so that most of it rests on the hands and head. Go directly into a Headstand, using a kick-up to achieve the inverted position. Maintain the triangle position of the hands and the head. In the final inverted position, the feet should be together, with legs straight and toes pointed. The weight is evenly distributed among the three points---the two hands and the forward part of the head. The body should be aligned as straight as possible.

The safest way to come down from the inverted position is to return to the mat in the direction that was used in going up. Recovery is helped by bending at both the waist and the knees. The child should be instructed, in the case of overbalancing, to tuck the head under and go into a Forward Roll. Both methods of recovery from the inverted position should be included in the instructional sequences early in the presentation.

Spotting the Headstand: The spotter is stationed directly in front of the performer and steadies as needed. The spotter can first apply support to the hips and then transfer to the ankles as the climb-up position is lengthened into a Headstand. If unable to control the performer, the spotter must be alert to moving out of the way when the performer goes into a Forward Roll to come out of the inverted position.

Backward Roll Combinations

Review the Backward Roll. Continue emphasis on the Push-Off with the hands. Try some of the following combinations:

1. Do a Backward Roll to a standing position. A strong push by the hands is necessary to provide enough momentum to land on the feet.
2. Do two Backward Rolls in succession.
3. Do a Crab Walk into a Backward Roll.
4. Add a jump in the air at the completion of a Backward Roll.

Balance Stunts

Long Reach

Place a beanbag about 3 feet in front of a line. Keeping the toes behind the line, lean forward on one hand and reach out with the other hand to touch the beanbag. Recover in one clean, quick movement to the original position, lifting the supporting hand off the floor. Increase the distance of the bag from the line.

Toe Jump

Hold the left toes with the right hand. Jump the right foot through without losing the grip on the toes. Try with the other foot. (Teachers should not be discouraged if only a few can do this stunt; it is quite difficult.)

Individual Stunts

Pretzel

Touch the back of the head with the toes by raising the head and trunk and bringing the feet to the back of the head. Try first to bring the toes close enough to the head so the head-to-toe distance can be measured by another child with a handspan (the distance between the thumb and little finger when spread). If this distance is met, then try touching one or both feet to the back of the head.

Jackknife

Stand erect with hands out level to the front and a little to the side. Jump up and bring the feet up quickly to touch the hands. Vary by starting with a short run. Be sure the feet come up to the hands, rather than the hands moving down to the feet. Do several Jackknives in succession. The takeoff must be with both feet, and good height must be achieved.

Heel-and-Toe Spring

Place the heels against a line. Jump backward over the line while bent over and grasping the toes. (Lean forward slightly to allow for impetus and then jump backward over the line.) Try jumping forward to original position. To be successful, the child should retain the grasp on the toes. The teacher can introduce the stunt by first having children grasp their ankles when making the jumps. This is less difficult.

Single-Leg Circle (Pinwheel)

Assume a squatting position, with both hands on the floor, left knee between the arms and right leg extended to the side. Swing the right leg forward and under the lifted right arm, under the left leg and arm, and back to starting position. Several circles should be made in succession. Reverse position and try with the left leg.

Partner and Group Stunts

Quintuplet Roll

Five children can make up a roll series. They are numbered 1 through 5. Numbers 3 and 5 begin by going over numbers 2 and 4, respectively, who roll under. Number 1 goes over number 3 as soon as possible. Each then continues to go alternately over and under.

Dead Person Lift

One child lies on her back, with body stiff and arms at the sides. Two helpers stand, one on each side of the "dead" person, with hands at the back of the neck and fingers touching. Working together, they lift the child, who remains rigid, to a standing position. From this position, the child is released and falls forward in a Dead Body Fall.

Injured Person Carry

The "injured" child lies on the back. Six children, three on each side, kneel down to do the carry. The lifters work their hands, palms upward, under the person to form a human stretcher, then lift up. (The "injured" child must maintain a stiff position.) They walk a short distance and set the person down carefully.

Merry-Go-Round

From 8 to 12 children are needed. Half of the children form a circle with joined hands, using a wrist grip. The remaining children drape themselves (each over a pair of joined hands) to become riders. The riders stretch out their bodies, faces up, toward the center of the circle, with the weight on the heels. Each rider then leans back on a pair of joined hands and connects hands, behind the circle of standing children, with the riders on either side. There are two sets of joined hands---the first circle, or merry-go-round, and the riders. The movement of the Merry-Go-Round is counterclockwise. The circle children, who provide the support, use sidesteps. The riders keep pace, taking small steps with their heels.

Combatives

Catch-and-Pull Tug-of-War

Starting Position: Two teams face each other across a line.

Action: Try to catch hold of and pull any opponent across the line. A player pulled across the line waits in back of the opposing team until time is called. The team capturing the most players wins.

Stick Twist

Starting Position: Contestants face each other with their feet approximately 12 inches apart. They hold a wand above their heads with both hands, the arms completely extended.

Action: On signal, try to bring the wand down slowly without changing the grip. The object is to maintain the original grip and not to let the wand twist in the hands. The wand does not have to be forced down, but rather should be moved down by mutual agreement. It can be moved down completely only if one player allows it to slip.

Toe Touch

Starting Position: Contestants form a large circle.

Action: On signal, try to step lightly on the opponent's toes (those on the left and right side) while not allowing the opponent to step on your toes. Keep score by counting the number of touches made.

Crab Contest

Starting Position: Both contestants are in crab position with seats held high.

Action: On signal, try, by jostling and pushing, to force the other's seat to touch the mat.

Game Activity

Pin Knockout

Supplies: Many playground balls, 12 bowling pins

Skills: Rolling, dodging

Two teams of equal number play the game. Each team is given many playground balls and six bowling pins. A court 30 by 60 ft or larger with a centerline is needed. The size of the court depends on the number of children in the game. The object of the game is to knock down all of the opponents' bowling pins. The balls are used for rolling at the opposing team's pins. Each team stays in its half of the court.

A player is eliminated if any of the following occurs:

1. She is touched by any ball at any time, regardless of the situation (other than picking up a ball).

2. She steps over the centerline to roll or retrieve a ball. (Any opposing team member hit as a result of such a roll is not eliminated.)

3. She attempts to block a rolling ball with a ball in her hands and the ball touches her in any manner.

A foul is called when a player holds a ball longer than 10 seconds without rolling at the opposing team. Play stops and the ball is given to the opposing team.

The bowling pins are put anywhere in the team's area. Players may guard the pins, but must not touch them. When pin is down, even though it might have been knocked over unintentionally by a member of the defending team, it is removed immediately from the game. The game is over when all pins on one side have been knocked down.

Over the Wall

Supplies: None

Skills: Running, dodging

Two parallel goal lines are drawn about 60 ft apart. Two additional parallel lines about 3 ft apart are laid out parallel to the goal lines in the middle of the game area. This is the wall. One player is it and stands on, or behind, the wall. All of the other players are behind one of the goal lines. The tagger calls "Over the wall." All of the players must then run across the wall to the other goal line. The child who is it tries to tag any player he can. Anyone caught helps catch the others. Players also are considered caught when they step on the wall. They must clear it with a leap or a jump and cannot step on it anywhere, including on the lines. After crossing over to the other side safely, players must wait for the next call. The game can be made more difficult by increasing the width of the wall. The taggers can step on or run through the wall at will.

Lesson Plans for Grades 5-6 - Week 23
Gymnastics (4)

Objectives:
To understand the principles of stability and balance
To control the body weight in a variety of tumbling and stunt activities
To participate in "one on one" competition and accept the outcome
To play group games and cooperate with teammates

Equipment Required:
Aerobic fitness tape
Tumbling mats
Foam rubber ball and pinnies for game

Instructional Activities	Teaching Hints

Introductory Activity -- Rubber Band

Students begin from a central point with the teacher. On signal, students move away from the teacher with a designated movement such as run, hop sideways, skip backward, double-lame dog, or Carioca. On signal, they sprint back to the central point.

An alternative way of doing rubber band is to give students 5 seconds to see how far they can move. On signal, they return and see if they reach the original point in 5 seconds.

Fitness Development Activity -- Parachute Fitness

1. Jog in circle with chute held in left hand. Reverse directions and hold with right hand.
2. Standing, raise the chute overhead, lower to waist, lower to toes, raise to waist, etc.
3. Slide to the right; return slide to the left.
4. Sit and perform curl-ups with a twist.
5. Skip.
6. Freeze, face the center, and stretch the chute tightly with bent arms. Hold for 8-12 seconds. Repeat.
7. Run in place, hold the chute at waist level, and hit the chute with lifted knees.
8. Sit with legs under the chute. Do a seat walk toward the center. Return to the perimeter. Repeat four to six times.
9. Place the chute on the ground. Jog away from the chute and return on signal. Repeat.
10. On sides with legs under the chute. Perform Side Flex and lift chute with legs.
11. Lie on back with legs under the chute. Shake the chute with the feet.
12. Hop to the center of the chute and return. Repeat.
13. Assume the push-up position with the legs aligned away from the center of the chute. Shake the chute with one arm while the other arm supports the body.
14. Sit with feet under the chute. Stretch by touching the toes with the chute. Relax with other stretches while sitting.

Tape alternating segments (25-30 seconds in length) of silence and music to signal duration of exercise. Music segments indicate aerobic activity with the parachute while intervals of silence announce using the chute to enhance flexibility and strength development.

Space youngsters evenly around the chute.

Use different hand grips (palms up, down, mixed).

All movements should be done under control. Some of the faster and stronger students will have to moderate their performance.

Lesson Focus – Gymnastics (4)

Five groups of activities in this lesson ensure that youngsters receive a variety of experiences. Pick a few activities from each group and teach them alternately. For example, teach an individual stunt or two, then a tumbling skill or inverted balance, followed by a balance stunt, etc. Give equal time to each group of activities

Review activities taught in previous gymnastics lesson plans.
   a. Tumbling and Inverted Balances
   b. Balance Stunts
   c. Individual Stunts
   d. Partner and Group Stunts
   e. Combatives

Game Activity

Octopus
   Supplies: None
   Skills: Maneuvering, problem solving
   Octopus is a game that gets its name from the many hands joined together in the activity. Children stand shoulder to shoulder in a tight circle. Everyone thrusts the hands forward and reaches through the group of hands to grasp the hands across the circle. Players must make sure that they do not hold both hands of the same player. Players also may not hold the hand of an adjacent player. The object is to untangle the mess created by the joined hands by going under, over, or through fellow players. No one is

permitted to release a hand grip during the unraveling. What is the end result? Perhaps one large circle or two smaller connected circles.

Teaching Suggestion: If, after a period of time, the knotted hands do not seem to unravel, call a halt and administer first aid. The teacher and group can decide where the difficulty is and allow a change in position of those hands until the know is dissolved. This should not be used as a competitive game because the difficulty of the knots cannot be equalized.

Fast Pass

Supplies: One 8-in. foam rubber ball, pinnies

Skills: Passing, catching, moving to an open area

One team begins with the ball. The object is to complete five consecutive passes without the ball touching the floor. The team without the ball attempts to intercept the ball or recover an incomplete pass. Each time a pass is completed, the team shouts the number of consecutive passes completed it represents. Each time a ball touches the floor or is intercepted, the count starts over.

Players may not contact each other. Emphasis should be placed on spreading out and using the entire court area. If players do not spread out, the area can be broken into quadrants and players restricted to one quadrant.

Lesson Plans for Grades 5-6 - Week 24
Manipulative Skills Using Wands and Hoops

Objectives:
To hear changes in the rhythm of music and move accordingly
To demonstrate activities designed to improve cardiovascular fitness
To manipulate hoops and wands in a variety of challenges

Equipment Required:
Tape for introductory activity and aerobic fitness
One wand and one hoop for each student
Cageball
12 yarnballs

Instructional Activities	Teaching Hints

Introductory Activity -- Moving to Music

Use different types of music to stimulate various locomotor and non-locomotor movements. Dance steps such as the polka, two-step, schottische and grapevine could be practiced.

If youngsters have trouble sensing the rhythm, use a tom-tom or tambourine to accentuate the beat

Fitness Development Activity -- Parachute Fitness

1. Jog in circle with chute held in left hand. Reverse directions and hold with right hand.
2. Standing, raise the chute overhead, lower to waist, lower to toes, raise to waist, etc.
3. Slide to the right; return slide to the left.
4. Sit and perform curl-ups with a twist.
5. Skip.
6. Freeze, face the center, and stretch the chute tightly with bent arms. Hold for 8-12 seconds. Repeat.
7. Run in place, hold the chute at waist level, and hit the chute with lifted knees.
8. Sit with legs under the chute. Do a seat walk toward the center. Return to the perimeter. Repeat four to six times.
9. Place the chute on the ground. Jog away from the chute and return on signal. Repeat.
10. On sides with legs under the chute. Perform Side Flex and lift chute with legs.
11. Lie on back with legs under the chute. Shake the chute with the feet.
12. Hop to the center of the chute and return. Repeat.
13. Assume the push-up position with the legs aligned away from the center of the chute. Shake the chute with one arm while the other arm supports the body.
14. Sit with feet under the chute. Stretch by touching the toes with the chute. Relax with other stretches while sitting.

Tape alternating segments (25-30 seconds in length) of silence and music to signal duration of exercise. Music segments indicate aerobic activity with the parachute while intervals of silence announce using the chute to enhance flexibility and strength development.

Space youngsters evenly around the chute.

Use different hand grips (palms up, down, mixed).

All movements should be done under control. Some of the faster and stronger students will have to moderate their performance.

Lesson Focus -- Manipulative Skills Using Wands and Hula Hoops

Select activities from the each of the exercises and challenges groups.

Strength Exercises with Wands

1. Pull the Wand Apart. Place the hands 6 inches apart near the center of the wand. With a tight grip to prevent slippage and with arms extended, pull the hands apart. Change grip and position.
2. Push the Wand Together. Hold the wand as previously, except push the hands together.
3. Wand Twist. Hold the wand with both hands about 6 inches apart. Twist the hands in opposite directions.
4. Bicycle. Holding the wand horizontally throughout and using an overhand grip, extend the wand outward and downward. Bring it upward near the body, completing a circular movement. On the downward movement, push the wand together, and on the upward movement, pull the wand apart.
5. Arm Spreader. Hold the wand overhead with hands spread wide. Attempt to compress the stick. Reverse force, and attempt to pull the stick apart.
6. Dead Lift. Partially squat and place the wand under the thighs. Place the hands between the legs and try to lift. Try also with hands on the outside of the legs.

Wands can be made from ¾ inch maple dowels or from a variety of broom and mop handles. They should be cut to a length of 36 inches. Wands are noisy when they hit the floor. Putting rubber crutch tips on the ends of a wand alleviates most of the noise and makes them easier to pick up.

The isometric exercises with wands presented can be performed with a variety of grips. With the wand horizontal, use either the overhand or underhand grip. With the wand in vertical position, grip with the thumbs pointed up, down, or toward each other.

7. Abdominal Tightener. From a standing position, place the wand behind the buttocks. With hands on the ends of the wand, pull forward and resist with the abdominal muscles.

Stretching Exercises with Wands

1. Side Bender. Grip the wand and extend the arms overhead with feet apart. Bend sideways as far as possible, maintaining straight arms and legs. Recover, and bend to the other side.
2. Body Twist. Place the wand behind the neck, with arms draped over the wand from behind. Rotate the upper body first to the right as far as possible and then to the left. The feet and hips should remain in position. The twist is at the waist.
3. Body Twist to Knee. Assume body twist position. Bend the trunk forward and twist so that the right end of the wand touches the left knee. Recover, and touch the left end to the right knee.
4. Shoulder Stretcher. Grip the wand at the ends in a regular grip. Extend the arms overhead and rotate the wand, arms, and shoulders backward until the stick touches the back of the legs. The arms should be kept straight. Those who find the stretch too easy should move their hands closer to the center of the wand.
5. Toe Touch. Grip the wand with the hands about shoulder width apart. Bend forward, reaching down as far as possible without bending the knees. The movement should be slow and controlled. Try the same activity from a sitting position.
6. Over the Toes. Sit down, flex the knees, place the wand over the toes, and rest it against the middle of the arch. Grip the stick with the fingers at the outside edge of the feet. Slowly extend the legs forward, pushing against the stick and trying for a full extension of the legs.

Wand Challenges

1. Can you reach down and pick up your wand without bending your knees?
2. Try to balance your wand on different body parts. Watch the top of the wand to get cues on how to retain the balance.
3. Can you hold your stick against the wall and move over it? Gradually raise the height of the wand.
4. Let's see whether you can hold the stick at both ends and move through the gap.
5. Put one end of the wand on the floor and hold the other end. How many times can you run around your wand without getting dizzy?
6. Place one end of the wand against a wall. Holding the other end and keeping the wand against the wall, duck underneath. Place the wand lower and lower on the wall and go under.
7. Toss the wand from one hand to the other.
8. Hold the wand vertically near the middle. Can you release your grip and catch the wand before it falls to the floor?
9. Have a partner hold a wand horizontally above the floor. Jump, leap, and hop over the wand. Gradually raise the height of the wand.
10. Balance the wand vertically on the floor. Release the wand and try to complete different stunts--clapping the hands, doing a heel click, touching different body parts--before the wand falls to the floor.

Hoop Activities

1. Hula-hoop using various body parts such as waist, neck, knees, arms and fingers.
    a. While hula-hooping on the arms, try to change the hoop from one arm to the other.
    b. Change hoop from one partner to another while hula-hooping.
    c. Try leg-skippers--hula-hoop with one leg and jump the hoop with the other leg.
2. Jump-rope with the hoop--forward, sideways, and backward. Begin with a back-and-forth swing.
3. Roll hoop and run alongside it. Run in front of it.
4. Roll hoop with a reverse spin to make it return to the thrower.
5. Roll with a reverse spin and see how many times partner can go through it.

Repeat each exercise with a different grip. Exercises can also be repeated with the wand in different positions: in front of the body (either horizontal or vertical), overhead, or behind the back. Hold each exercise for 8 to 12 seconds.

Be gentle when stretching. Reach and stretch the muscles, hold the stretch for a few seconds and relax. Repeat a number of times.

Because wands are noisy when dropped, youngsters should hold their wands with both hands or put them on the floor during instruction.

An adequate amount of space is needed for each individual, because wand stunts demand room.

Children may easily be injured using wands improperly. Teach children proper use of wands. Emphasize the need to use care when handling wands to avoid injury to self and others. Do not allow any improper use of wands.

Hoops produce noisy activity. The teacher may find it helpful to have the children lay their hoops on the floor when they are to listen.

The key to the reverse spin is to pull down (toward the floor) on the hoop as it is released

6. Roll the hoop with a reverse spin, jump over it, and catch it as it returns. Roll the hoop with a reverse spin, and as it returns, hoist it with the foot and catch it. Roll the hoop with a reverse spin, kick it up with the toe, and go through the hoop. Roll the hoop with a reverse spin, run around it, and catch it. Roll the hoop with a reverse spin, pick it up, and begin hooping on the arm---all in one motion.

7. Balance the hoop on your head, try to walk through it ("thread the needle") forward, backward and sideways.

8. Try partner activities:
   a. Play catch with hoop.
   b. Hula-hoop on one arm, toss to partner who catches it on one arm.
   c. Use two hoops for catching.
   d. Hoop with one hoop and play catch with other.
   e. Move through a hoop held by a partner.

When teaching the reverse spin with hoops, have the students throw the hoop up, in place, rather than forward along the floor. After they learn the upward throw, they can progress to the forward throw for distance.

Game Activity

Galactic Empire and Rebels

Supplies: None

Skills: Chasing, fleeing, dodging

This game can be played indoors or outdoors in a square that is approximately 100 ft on each side. Each team's spaceport is behind the end line, where the single space fighters are stationed, waiting to issue against the enemy. To begin, one or more space fighters from either team move from their spaceport to entice enemy fliers for possible capture. A flyer leaving the spaceport may capture only opposing flyers who previously have left their respective spaceport. This is the basic rule of the game. A flyer may go back to his spaceport and be eligible immediately to issue again to capture an opponent who was already in general space. The technique of the game is to entice enemy flyers close to the spaceport so that fellow flyers can issue and capture (tag) an opposing flyer.

As an illustration of how the game proceeds: Rebel flyer 1 moves into general space to entice Empire flyer 1 so that he can be captured. Rebel flyer 1 turns back and heads for her spaceport, chased by Empire flyer 1. Rebel flyer 2 now leaves her spaceport and tags Empire flyer 1 before the Empire flyer can tag Rebel flyer 1. The Empire flyer is now a prisoner.

A player captured by an opposing flyer is taken to the tagger's prison--both captor and captive are given free passage to the prison. In prison, the captives form a chain gang, holding hands and extending the prisoners' line toward their own spaceport. The last captive is always at the end of the prisoners' line with one foot in the prison. Captives can be released if a teammate can get to them without being tagged. The released prisoner (only the end one) is escorted back to her own spaceport and both players are given free passage.

The game becomes one of capturing opposing flyers and securing the release of captured teammates. Flyers stepping over the sideline automatically become prisoners. One or two players in the spaceport should be assigned to guard the prison.

Set a time limit of 10 minutes for the contest, and declare the team with the most prisoners the winner.

Jolly Ball

Supplies: A cageball 24 in. or larger (or a 36- to 48 inch pushball)

Skill: Kicking

Four teams are organized, each of which forms one side of a hollow square. Children sit down, facing in, with hands braced behind them (crab position). The members of each team are numbered consecutively. Each child waits until his number is called. Four active players (one from each team) move in crab position and try to kick the cageball over any one of the three opposing teams. The sideline players can also kick the ball. Ordinarily, the hands are not used, but this could be allowed in the learning stages of the game.

A point is scored against a team that allows the ball to go over its line. A ball that goes out at the corner between teams is dead and must be replayed. When a point is scored, the active children retire to their teams and another number is called. The team with the fewest points wins the game. This game is quite strenuous for the active players, so they should be rotated after a reasonable length of time when there is no score.

Variation: Two children from each team can be active at once.

Circle Touch

Supplies: Yarnballs

Skills: Dodging, body management

One child plays against three others, who form a small circle with joined hands. The object of the game is for the lone child to touch a designated child (on the shoulders) in the circle with a yarnball. The other two children in the circle, by dodging and maneuvering, attempt to keep the tagger away from the third member of the circle. The circle players may maneuver and circle in any direction but must not release hand grips. The tagger, in attempting to touch the protected circle player, must go around the outside of the circle. She is not permitted to go underneath or through the joined hands of the circle players. To avoid roughness, the game should be played in short 20 second bouts and then rotate in a new tagger.

Lesson Plans for Grades 5-6 - Week 25
Volleyball Skills (1)

Objectives:
To lead and follow aerobic activities with a partner
To serve a volleyball in a predetermined direction
To understand basic principles of training

Equipment Required:
One beanbag per student
One volleyball trainer or foam training
    ball for each student
Volleyball net

Instructional Activities	Teaching Hints

Introductory Activity -- Vanishing Beanbags

Beanbags (one per student) are spread throughout the area. Students move throughout the area. On signal, they find a beanbag and sit on it. On the next signal or command, the students move again, with a few beanbags being removed during the interval. On signal, they once again sit on a beanbag. The object is to try not to be left without a beanbag move than five times.

There are no ties when finding a beanbag to sit on. If students feel it is a tie, both must leave that bag and find another.

Specify placing different body parts on the beanbag.

Fitness Development Activity -- Partner Aerobic Fitness and Resistance Exercises

Students find a partner and lead each other in aerobic activities. Partners switch leader and follower roles after each partner resistance exercise. This routine assumes that students have previous aerobic fitness experience. See text, p. 195-199 for descriptions of aerobic activities.

Bounce and Clap	25 seconds
Arm Curl-Up	45 seconds
Jumping Jack variations	25 seconds
Camelback	45 seconds
Lunge variations	25 seconds
Fist Pull apart	45 seconds
Directional Runs	25 seconds
Scissors	45 seconds
Rhythmic Running	25 seconds
Butterfly	45 seconds
Bounce with Body Twist	25 seconds
Resistance Push-Up	45 seconds

Walk, stretch and relax for a minute or two.

Tape alternating segments of silence and music to signal duration of exercise. Music segments indicate aerobic activity (25 seconds) while intervals of silence announce partner resistance exercises (45 seconds).

Teach the exercises first. See text, p. 187-189 for descriptions of partner resistance activities. A sign with aerobic activities on one side and partner resistance exercises on the other help students remember the activities. The signs can be held upright by cones and shared by 2-4 students.

Take 6-10 seconds to complete a resistance exercise.

Lesson Focus -- Volleyball Skills, Drills, and Lead-Up Games (1)

Skills
Practice the following skills:
Overhand Pass

    To execute an overhand pass, the player moves underneath the ball and controls it with the fingertips. The cup of the fingers is made so that the thumbs and forefingers are close together and the other fingers are spread. The hands are held forehead high, with elbows out and level with the floor. The player, when in receiving position, looks ready to shout upward through the hands. The player contacts the ball above eye level and propels it with the force of spread fingers, not with the palms. At the moment of contact, the legs are straightened and the hands and arms follow through.

Forearm Pass (Underhand Pass)

    The hands are clasped together so that the forearms are parallel. The clasp should be relaxed, with the type of handclasp a matter of choice. The thumbs are kept parallel and together, and the fingers of one hand make a partially cupped fist, with the fingers of the other hand overlapping the fist. The wrists are turned downward and the elbow joints are reasonably locked. The forearms are held at the proper angle to rebound the ball, with contact made with the fists or forearms between the knees as the receiver crouches.

Using trainer volleyballs will allow youngsters time to move into the path of the volleyball instead of reaching for the ball. Proper footwork is critical to the success of volleyball; using proper balls will help assure that youngsters learn correctly.

Instructional cues for passing include the following:
1. Move into the path of the ball; don't reach for it.
2. Bend the knees prior to making contact.
3. Contact the ball with the fingertips (overhand pass).
4. Extend the knees upon contact with the ball.
5. Follow through after striking the ball.

Underhand Serve

Directions are for a right-handed serve. The player stands facing the net with the left foot slightly forward and the weight on the right (rear) foot. The ball is held in the left hand with the left arm across and a little in front of the body. On the serving motion, the server steps forward with the left foot, transferring the weight to the front foot, and at the same time brings the right arm back in a preparatory motion. The right hand now swings forward and contacts the ball just below center. The ball can be hit with an open hand or with the fist (facing forward or sideward). Children should explore the best way to strike the ball, with the flat of the hand or the fist. Each player can select the method that is personally most effective.

Setup

The term setup applies to a pass that sets the ball for a possible spike. The object is to raise the ball with a soft, easy pass to a position 1 or 2 feet above the net and about 1 foot away from it. The setup is generally the second pass in a series of three. An overhand pass is used for the setup. It is important for the back line player, who has to tap to the setter, to make an accurate and easily handled pass.

Individual Passing Drills

1. Practice wall rebounding: Stand 6 feet away from a wall. Pass the ball against the wall and catch it.
2. From a spot 6 feet from the wall, throw the ball against the wall and alternate an overhand pass with a forearm pass.
3. Throw the ball to one side (right or left) and move to the side to pass the ball to the wall. Catch the rebound.
4. Pass the ball directly overhead and catch it. Try making two passes before catching the ball. Later, alternate an overhand pass with a forearm pass and catch the ball.

Partner Passing Drills

1. Players are about 10 feet apart. Play A tosses the ball (controlled toss) to player B, who passes the ball back to A, who catches the ball. Continue for several exchanges and then change throwers.
2. Two players are about 15 feet apart. Player a passes to themselves first and then makes a second pass to player B, who catches the ball and repeats. Follow with a return by B.
3. Players A and B try to keep the ball in the air continuously.
4. Players are about 15 feet apart. Player A remains stationary and passes in such a fashion that player B must move from side to side. An option is to have player B move forward and backward.
5. Players are about 10 feet apart. Both have hoops and attempt to keep one foot in the hoop while passing. Try keeping both feet in the hoop.
6. Player A passes to player B and does a complete turnaround. B passes back to A and also does a full turn. Other stunts can be used.

Partner Work (Serving and Passing)

1. Partners are about 20 feet apart. Partner A serves to partner B, who catches the ball and returns the serve to partner A.
2. Partner A serves to partner B, who makes a pass back to partner A. Change responsibilities.
3. Service One-Step. Partners begin about 10 feet apart. Partner A serves to partner B, who returns the serve with partner A catching. If there is no error and if neither receiver moved the feet to catch, both players take one step back. This is repeated each time no error or foot movement by the receivers occur. If an error occurs or if appreciable foot movement is evident, the players revert to the original distance of 10 feet and start over.
4. A player stands at the top of the key on a basketball court. The object is to serve the ball into the basket. Scoring can be as in other basket-making drills: 3 points for a basket, 2 points for hitting the rim, and 1 point for hitting the backboard but not the rim. Partner retrieves the ball.

Instructional cues for the serve:
1. Use opposition. Place the opposite foot of the serving hand forward.
2. Transfer the weight to the forward foot.
3. Keep the eyes on the ball.
4. Decide prior to the serve where it should be placed.
5. Follow through; don't punch at the ball.

The usual basketball court should be divided into two volleyball courts on which players play crosswise. Nets should be lowered to 6 feet and raised 6 to 12 inches as children mature.

In the Air

Supplies: A trainer volleyball for each team

Skills: Overhand, forearm, and dig passes

Each team forms a small circle of not more than eight players. The object of the game is to see which team can make the greater number of volleys in a specified time or which team can keep the ball in the air for the greater number of consecutive volleys without error.

On the signal "Go," the game is started with a volley by one of the players. The following rules are in force.

1. Balls are volleyed back and forth with no specific order of turns, except that the ball cannot be returned to the player from whom it came.

2. A player may not volley a ball twice in succession.

3. Any ball touching the ground does not count and ends the count.

Teaching suggestions: Players should be responsible for calling illegal returns on themselves and thus interrupting the consecutive volley count. The balls used should be of equal quality, so that one team cannot claim a disadvantage. Groups should be taught to count the volleys out loud, so that their progress is known.

Mini-Volleyball

Supplies: A volleyball or trainer volleyball

Skills: Most volleyball skills

Mini-Volleyball is a modified activity designed to offer opportunities for successful volleyball experiences to children between the ages of 9 and 12. The playing area is 15 ft wide and 40 ft long. The spiking line is 10 ft from the centerline. Many gymnasiums are marked for badminton courts that are 20 by 44 ft with a spiking line 6.5 ft from the center. This is an acceptable substitute court.

The modified rules used in Mini-Volleyball are as follows.

1. A team consists of three players. Two substitutions may be made per game.

2. Players are positioned for the serve so that there are two front-line players and one back-line player. After the ball is served, the back-line player may not spike the ball from the attack area or hit the ball into the attack area unless the ball is below the height of the net.

3. The height of the net is 6 ft, 10 in.

4. Players rotate positions when they receive the ball for serving. The right front-line player becomes the back-line player, and the left front-line player becomes the right front-line player.

5. A team wins a game when it scores 15 points and has a 2-point advantage over the opponent. A team wins the match when it wins two out of three games.

The back-line player cannot spike and thus serves a useful function by allowing the front players to receive the serves while he moves to the net to set up for the spikers.

Teaching suggestion: This game can be modified to suit the needs of participants. Sponge training balls work well in the learning stages of Mini-Volleyball.

Regulation Volleyball

Supplies: A volleyball

Skills: All volleyball skills

Regulation volleyball should be played with one possible rule change: In early experiences, it is suggested that the server be allowed a second chance if she fails to get the first attempt over the net and into play. This should apply only to the initial serve. Some instructors like to shorten the serving distance during the introductory phases of the game. It is important for the serving to be done well enough to keep the game moving.

A referee should supervise the game. There are generally three calls.

1. "Side out." The serving team fails to serve the ball successfully to the other court, fails to make a good return of a volley, or makes a rule violation.

2. "Point." The receiving team fails to make a legal return or is guilty of a rule violation.

3. "Double foul." Fouls are made by both teams on the same play, in which case the point is replayed. No score or side out results.

Teaching suggestion: There should be some emphasis on team play. Backcourt players should be encouraged to pass to front court players rather than merely batting the ball back and forth across the net.

Lesson Plans for Grades 5-6 - Week 26
Volleyball Skills (2)

Objectives:
To evade a partner by moving under control and dodging
To show respect for peers with different skill levels
To accept decisions made by officials

Equipment Required:
One volleyball trainer or foam training
ball for each student
Volleyball net

Instructional Activities	Teaching Hints

Introductory Activity -- Marking

Each child has a partner who is somewhat equal in ability. Under control, one partner runs, dodges, and tries to lose the other, who must stay within 3 feet of the runner. On signal, both stop. Chasers must be able to touch their partners to say that they have marked them. Partners then change roles.

Allow a point to be scored only when they touch a specified body part (i.e., knee, elbow, left hand).

Fitness Development Activity -- Partner Aerobic Fitness and Resistance Exercises

Students find a partner and lead each other in aerobic activities. Partners switch leader and follower roles after each partner resistance exercise. This routine assumes that students have previous aerobic fitness experience. See text, p. 195-199 for descriptions of aerobic activities.

Bounce and Clap	25 seconds
Arm Curl-Up	45 seconds
Jumping Jack variations	25 seconds
Camelback	45 seconds
Lunge variations	25 seconds
Fist Pull apart	45 seconds
Directional Runs	25 seconds
Scissors	45 seconds
Rhythmic Running	25 seconds
Butterfly	45 seconds
Bounce with Body Twist	25 seconds
Resistance Push-Up	45 seconds

Walk, stretch and relax for a minute or two.

Tape alternating segments of silence and music to signal duration of exercise. Music segments indicate aerobic activity (25 seconds) while intervals of silence announce partner resistance exercises (45 seconds).

Teach the exercises first. See text, p. 187-189 for descriptions of partner resistance activities. A sign with aerobic activities on one side and partner resistance exercises on the other help students remember the activities. The signs can be held upright by cones and shared by 2-4 students.

Take 6-10 seconds to complete a resistance exercise.

Lesson Focus -- Volleyball Skills, Drills, and Lead-Up Games (2)

Skills
Review the skills learned last week. Use some of the drills introduced in the previous lesson to practice the skills.
- a. Underhand serve
- b. Overhand pass
- c. Serving
- d. Setup

Introduce a new skill.
Blocking
    A member of the defensive team forms a screen by extending hands and arms straight up while jumping straight up. The ball is not struck, but rebounds from the blocker's stiffened hands and arms.

Drills
Leave time for playing volleyball lead-up games.
Station (Small Group) Instruction
Divide the class into four equal groups. Set up a system of rotation that assures all stations will be covered.

Blocking involves one or more members of the defensive (receiving) team forming a screen of arms and hands near the net to block a spike. At the elementary school level, blocking is usually done by a single individual, and little attention is given to multiple blocking. To block a ball, a player jumps high with arms outstretched overhead, palms facing the net, and fingers spread. The jump must be timed with that of the spiker, and the blocker must avoid touching the net. The ball is not struck but rather rebounds from the blocker's stiffened hands and arms. Students should know about blocking even if it is used infrequently in elementary play.

Station 1 - Individual Volleying

1. Volley the ball directly overhead and catch. Try to consecutive volleys before the catch. Next, alternate a bump with an overhand pass before the catch. Finally, try to keep the ball going five or six times in a row with one kind of volley; alternate kinds of volleys.

2. Volley the ball 15 feet overhead, make a full turn and pass the ball again. Vary with other stunts (i.e., touching the floor, a heel click, clapping the hands at two different spots).

Station 2 - Volleying with a Partner

Players are 10 feet apart. One player tosses the ball to the other, who volleys it back to the first player, who catches it. After several volleys by one player, exchange tossers. Players can try to keep the ball going back and forth with a designated number of volleys before one player catches the ball.

Station 3 - Serving to a Partner

One partner serves to the other, who volleys the ball back. Exchange responsibilities after several serves and return volleys.

Station 4 - Setting and Blocking

For blocking, three players are positioned alongside the net, each with a ball. The players take turns on the other side of the net, practicing blocking skills. Each spiker tosses the ball to himself for spiking. A defensive player moves along the line to block consecutively a total of three spikes. The next step is to have two players move along the line to practice blocking by pairs.

Station work is facilitated if signs are made directing students what to do at each station. List key points and how to do the drills. Signs allow students to work independently

Many of the drills can be done without a net. This allows better use of space since nets restrict how much of the area is used.

Game Activity

Mini-Volleyball

See Volleyball Skills, Lesson 1 (p. 64) for a complete game description.

Regulation Volleyball

See Volleyball Skills, Lesson 1 (p. 64) for a complete game description.

Three and Over Volleyball

Supplies: A volleyball

Skills: All volleyball skills

The game Three and Over emphasizes the basic offensive strategy of volleyball. The game follows regular volleyball rules with the exception that the ball must be played three times before going over the net. The team loses the serve or the point if the ball is not played three times.

Rotation Mini-Volleyball

Supplies: A volleyball

Skills: All volleyball skills

If four teams are playing in two contests at the same time, a system of rotation can be set up during any one class period. Divide the available class time roughly into three parts, less the time allotted for logistics. Each team plays the other three teams on a timed basis. At the end of a predetermined time period, whichever team is ahead wins the game. A team may win, lose, or tie during any time period, with the score determined at the end of the respective time period. The best win-loss record wins the overall contest.

Lesson Plans for Grades 5-6 - Week 27
Rhythmic Movement (3)

Objectives:
To develop personal aerobic fitness activities
To perform locomotor movements to rhythm
To understand strategies in simple game activities

Equipment Required:
Tinkling poles
Music for rhythmic activities
Pinnies
6 playground balls
Jump the shot rope

Instructional Activities	Teaching Hints

Introductory Activity -- Move and Perform Athletic Movement

Students move and stop on signal. They then perform an athletic skill move, such as a basketball jump shot, leaping football pass catch, volleyball spike, or soccer kick. Students should place emphasis on correct form and timing.

A variation of the activity is to move with a partner and throw a pass on signal, punt a ball, or shoot a basket. The partner catches the ball or rebounds the shot.

Fitness Development Activity -- Partner Aerobic Fitness and Resistance Exercises

Students find a partner and lead each other in aerobic activities. Partners switch leader and follower roles after each partner resistance exercise. This routine assumes that students have previous aerobic fitness experience. See text, p. 195-199 for descriptions of aerobic activities.

Bounce and Clap	25 seconds
Arm Curl-Up	45 seconds
Jumping Jack variations	25 seconds
Camelback	45 seconds
Lunge variations	25 seconds
Fist Pull apart	45 seconds
Directional Runs	25 seconds
Scissors	45 seconds
Rhythmic Running	25 seconds
Butterfly	45 seconds
Bounce with Body Twist	25 seconds
Resistance Push-Up	45 seconds

Walk, stretch and relax for a minute or two.

Tape alternating segments of silence and music to signal duration of exercise. Music segments indicate aerobic activity (25 seconds) while intervals of silence announce partner resistance exercises (45 seconds).

Teach the exercises first; See text, p. 187-189 for descriptions of partner resistance activities. A sign with aerobic activities on one side and partner resistance exercises on the other help students remember the activities. The signs can be held upright by cones and shared by 2-4 students.

Take 6-10 seconds to complete a resistance exercise.

Lesson Focus -- Rhythmic Movement (3)

Make dances easy for students to learn by implementing some of the following techniques:
Rhythms should be taught like other sport skills. Avoid striving for perfection so students know it is acceptable to make mistakes. Teach a variety of dances rather than one or two in depth in case some students find it difficult to master a specific dance.
    1. Teach the dances without using partners.
    2. Allow youngsters to move in any direction without left-right orientation.
    3. Use scattered formation instead of circles.
    4. Emphasize strong movements such as clapping and stamping to increase involvement.
    5. Play the music at a slower speed when first learning the dance.

When introducing a dance, use the following methodology:
    1. Tell about the dance and listen to the music.
    2. Clap the beat and learn the verse.
    3. Practice the dance steps without the music and with verbal cues.
    4. Practice the dance with the music.

Records can be ordered from Wagon Wheel Records, 17191 Corbina Lane #203, Huntington Beach, CA (714) 846-8169.

Jugglehead Mixer (American)

Records: Any music with a definite and steady beat
Formation: Double circle facing counterclockwise in promenade position
Directions: Actions described are for the inside partner; directions are opposite for the partner on the outside of the circle.

Measures	Action
1--4	Do a two-step left and two-step right and take four walking steps forward.
5--8	Repeat measures 1--4.
9--10	Inside partner takes the outside partner's right hand and walks around to face the person behind.
11--12	Inside partner turns the person behind with the left hand.
13--14	Inside partner turns partner with the right hand going all the way around.
15--16	Inside partner steps up one place to the outside person ahead, who becomes the new partner.

Ten Pretty Girls (American)

Record: EZ 5003
Formation: Circle of groups of any number, with arms linked or hands joined, all facing counterclockwise
Directions:

Measures	Action
1--2	Starting with the weight on the right foot, touch the left foot in front, swing the left foot to the left and touch, swing the left foot behind the right foot and put the weight on the left foot, step to the right, close the left foot to the right. (Front, side, back-side, together)
3--4	Repeat, starting with the weight on the left foot and moving to the right. (Front, side, back-side, together)
5--6	Take four walking or strutting steps forward, starting on the left foot. (Walk, 2, 3, 4)
7--8	Swing the left foot forward with a kicking motion; swing the left foot backward with a kicking motion; stamp left, right, left, in place. (Swing, swing, stamp, stamp, stamp)

Repeat the entire dance 11 times, starting each time with the alternate foot. The dance can be used as a mixer when performed in a circle by groups of three. On measures 7--8, have the middle person move forward to the next group during the three stamps.

Klumpakojis (Swedish)

Record: MAV 1042
Formation: Couples in a circle, side by side, all facing counterclockwise, with partner B to the right
Directions:

Measures	Part I Action
1--4	With inside hands joined, free hand on hip, all walk briskly around the circle for eight steps counterclockwise. (Walk, 2, 3, 4, 5, 6, 7, turn)
5--8	Turn individually to the left, reverse direction, change hands, and walk eight steps clockwise. (Walk, 2, 3, 4, 5, 6, 7, turn)

Measures	Part II Action
9--12	Face partner and make a star by joining right hands (making certain that the right elbow is bent). The left hand is on the hip. With partner, walk around clockwise for eight walking steps. Change hands and repeat the eight steps, reversing direction. (Star, 2, 3, 4, 5, 6, 7, 8; Reverse, 2, 3, 4, 5, 6, 7, 8)

Measures	Part III Action
13--16	Listen to the musical phrase, then stamp three times on the last two counts. Listen to the phrase again, then clap own hands three times. (Listen, listen, stamp, 2, 3; Listen, listen, clap, 2, 3)
17--20	Shake the right finger in a scolding motion at partner. (Scold, 2, 3) Shake the left finger. (Scold, 2, 3)
21--24	Turn solo to the left, clapping partner's right hand once during the turn. Use two walking steps to make the turn, and finish facing partner. (Turn, 2, stamp, 2, 3)
25--32	Repeat the action of measures 13—24.

Measures	Part IV Action
33--40	With inside hands joined, do 16 polka steps (or two-steps) forward, moving counterclockwise. (Later, as the dance is learned, change to the promenade position.) On polka steps 15 and 16, partner A moves forward to take a new partner B while handing the original partner B to the A in back. New couple joins inside hands. (Step, close, step, hop; Step, close, step, hop; Repeat for a total of 16 polka steps)

Tinikling (Philippine Islands)

Records: KIM 8095, 9015; MAV 1047
Formation: Sets of fours scattered around the room. Each set has two strikers and two dancers.
Directions:

Two 8-foot bamboo poles and two crossbars on which the poles rest are needed for the dance. A striker kneels at each end of the poles; both strikers hold the end of a pole in each hand. The music is in waltz meter, 3/4 time, with an accent on the first beat. The strikers slide and strike the poles together on count 1. On the other two beats of the waltz measure, the poles are opened about 15 inches apart, lifted an inch or so, and tapped twice on the crossbars in time to counts 2 and 3. The rhythm "close, tap, tap" is continued throughout the dance, each sequence constituting a measure.

Basically, the dance requires that a step be done outside the poles on the close (count 1) and that two steps be done inside the poles (counts 2 and 3) when the poles are tapped on the crossbars. Many step combinations have been devised. The basic tinikling step should be practiced until it is mastered. The step is done singly, although two dancers are performing. Each dancer takes a position at an opposite end and on the opposite side so that the dancer's right side is to the bamboo poles.

Count 1: Step slightly forward with the left foot.
Count 2: Step with the right foot between the poles.
Count 3: Step with the left foot between the poles.
Count 4: Step with the right outside to dancer's own right.
Count 5: Step with the left between the poles.
Count 6: Step with the right between the poles.
Count 7: Step with the left outside to the original position.

The initial step (count 1) is used only to get the dance under way. The last step (count 7) to original position is actually the beginning of a new series (7, 8, 9--10, 11, 12).

Tinikling steps also can be adjusted to 4/4 rhythm (close, close, tap, tap), which requires the poles to be closed on two counts and open on the other two. The basic foot pattern is two steps outside the poles and two inside. For the sake of conformity, we present all routines in the original 3/4 time (close, tap, tap). If other rhythms are used, adjust accordingly.

Dancers can go from side to side, or can return to the side from which they entered. The dance can be done singly, with the two dancers moving in opposite directions from side to side, or the dancers can enter from and leave toward the same side. Dancers can do the same step patterns or do different movements. They can dance as partners, moving side by side with inside hands joined, or facing each other with both hands joined.

Teaching suggestions:

Steps should be practiced first with stationary poles or with lines drawn on the floor. Jump ropes can be used as stationary objects over which to practice. Students handling the poles should concentrate on watching each other rather than the dancer to avoid becoming confused by the dancer's feet.

To gain a sense of the movement pattern for 3/4 time, slap both thighs with the hands on the "close," and clap the hands twice for movements inside the poles. For 4/4 time, slap the right thigh with the right hand, then the left thigh with the left hand, followed by two claps. This routine should be done to music, with the poles closing and opening as indicated. Getting the feel of the rhythm is important.

Game Activity

Whistle Ball

Supplies: A ball for each group of six to eight players

Skills: Passing, catching

Eight or fewer children stand in circle formation. A ball is passed rapidly back and forth among them in any order. The object is to be the player who stays in the game the longest. A child sits down in place if he makes any of the following errors:

1. He has the ball when the whistle blows. (The teacher should set a predetermined time period, at the end of which a whistle is blown. The time period can be varied from 5 to 20 seconds.)

2. He makes a bad throw or fails to catch a good throw.

3. He returns the ball directly to the person from whom it was received.

Teaching suggestion: One way to control the time periods is to appoint a child as timer and to give her a list of the time periods, a whistle, and a stopwatch. The timer should be cautioned not to give any advance indication of when the stop signal will be blown. An automatic timer enhances the game. When the game gets down to two or three players, declare them the winners and begin anew.

Jump the Shot Variations

Supplies: A jump-the-shot rope

Skill: Rope jumping

Before the following variations are tried, the jump-the-shot routines and variations taught previously should be reviewed.

1. Two or more squads are in file formation facing the rope turner. Each player runs clockwise (against the turn of the rope), jumping the rope as often as necessary to return to the squad.

2. Each player runs counterclockwise and tries to run around the circle before the rope can catch up with him. If this happens, he must jump to allow the rope to go under him. The best time for a player to start his run is just after the rope has passed.

3. Players can try some of the stunts in which the hands and feet are on the ground, to see whether they can have the rope pass under them. The Rabbit Jump, push-up position, Lame Dog, and others are possibilities.

Lesson Plans for Grades 5-6 - Week 28
Rhythmic Movement (4)

Objectives:
To develop an appreciation of folk dances and their respective cultures
To cooperate in a social setting (folk dancing)
To jump a self-turned rope for an extended period of time

Equipment Required:
One individual jump rope for each
  student
15 scooters
Small object for Touchdown game

Instructional Activities	Teaching Hints

Introductory Activity -- Popcorn

Student pair up with one person on the floor in push-up position and the other standing ready to move. On signal, the standing students move over and under the persons on the floor. The person on the floor changes from a raised to a lowered push-up position each time the partner goes over or under them. On signal, reverse positions.

Remind students not to touch others when moving over and under.

Push-up challenges can be done in lieu of push-ups.

Fitness Development Activity -- Continuity Drills

See Lesson Plan 12, p. 27-28 for a description of all the rope jumping steps. See text, p. 174-186 for descriptions of exercises.

Rope jumping—forward	25 seconds
Double Crab Kick	30 seconds
Rope jumping—backward	25 seconds
Knee Touch Curl-Up	30 seconds
Jump and turn body	25 seconds
Push-Ups	30 seconds
Rocker Step	25 seconds
Bend and Twist	30 seconds
Swing -Step forward	25 seconds
Side Flex	30 seconds
Free jumping	25 seconds

Relax and stretch for a short time.

Make a tape with music segments (25 seconds) alternated with silence segments (30 seconds). When the music is playing, students jump rope; when silence occurs, students do a flexibility and strength development exercise.

Exercises can be done in two-count fashion. Exercises are done when the leader says "Ready." The class answers "One-two" and performs a repetition.

Allow students to adjust the workload to their level. This implies resting if the rope jumping is too strenuous.

Lesson Focus -- Rhythmic Movement (4)

Make dances easy for students to learn by implementing some of the following techniques:
Rhythms should be taught like other sport skills. Avoid striving for perfection so students know it is acceptable to make mistakes. Teach a variety of dances rather than one or two in depth in case some students find it difficult to master a specific dance.
  1. Teach the dances without using partners.
  2. Allow youngsters to move in any direction without left-right orientation.
  3. Use scattered formation instead of circles.
  4. Emphasize strong movements such as clapping and stamping to increase involvement.
  5. Play the music at a slower speed when first learning the dance.

When introducing a dance, use the following methodology:
  1. Tell about the dance and listen to the music.
  2. Clap the beat and learn the verse.
  3. Practice the dance steps without the music and with verbal cues.
  4. Practice the dance with the music.

Records can be ordered from Wagon Wheel Records, 17191 Corbina Lane #203, Huntington Beach, CA (714) 846-8169.

Jiffy Mixer

Records: KIM 1146; Windsor 4684
Formation: Double circle, partners facing.
Directions: The Windsor record has an introduction. Directions are for partners A; B's actions are opposite.

Introduction---use with Windsor record only

1--4   Wait, wait, balance apart (push away on the left foot and touch the right). Balance together (forward on the right and touch the left).

Measures **Action**

1--4   Strike the left heel diagonally out and return to touch the toe near the right foot. Repeat. Do a side step left with a touch. (Heel, toe; Heel, toe; Side, close; Side, touch)

5--8   Repeat while moving in the opposite direction, beginning with the right foot. (Heel, toe; Heel, toe; Side, close; Side, touch)

9--12   Take four chug steps backward clapping on the up beat. (Chug, clap, chug, clap, chug, clap, chug, clap)

13--16   Starting with the left foot, take four slow, swaggering steps diagonally to the right, progressing to a new partner. (Walk, 2, 3, 4)

The chug step is done by jumping and dragging both feet backward. The body is bent slightly forward.

Horse and Buggy Schottische (American)

Records: MAC 5003; LS E-14; RPT 108

Formation: Couples in sets of four in a double circle, facing counterclockwise. Couples join inside hands and give outside hands to the other couple (Figure 16.10).

Directions:

Measures **Action**

1--2   Moving forward, perform two schottische steps. (Step, step, step, hop; Step, step, step, hop)

3--4   Progress in line of direction performing four step-hops. (Step-hop, 2-hop, 3-hop, 4-hop)

During the four step-hops, either of the following patterns can be done.

    1. The lead couple drops inside hands and step-hops around the outside of the back couple, who move forward during the step-hops. The lead couple then joins hands behind the other couple, and the positions are reversed.

    2. The lead couple continues to hold hands and move backward under the upraised hands of the back couple, who untwist by turning away from each other.

Alunelul (Romanian)

Records: WT 10005; CM 1162

Formation: Single circle, hands on shoulders to both sides, arms straight ("T" position)

Directions: The Romanians are famous for rugged dances. This dance is called "Little Hazelnut." The stomping action represents the breaking of the hazelnuts. The title is pronounced "ah-loo-NAY-loo."

Measures **Part I Action**

1--2   Sidestep right, step left behind right, sidestep right, step left behind right, sidestep right, stomp left foot twice. (Side, back, side, back, side, stomp, stomp)

3--4   Beginning with the left foot, repeat the action but with reverse footwork. (Side, back, side, back, side, stomp, stomp)

5--8   Repeat the action of measures 1--4.

Measures **Part II Action**

9--10   Sidestep right, left behind right, sidestep right, stomp. (Side, back, side, stomp)

11--12   Sidestep left, right behind left, sidestep left, stomp. (Side, back, side, stomp)

13--16   Repeat the action of measures 9--12.

Measures **Part III Action**

17--18   In place, step right, stomp left; step left, stomp right; step right, stomp left twice. (Side, stomp, side, stomp, side, stomp)

19--20   In place, step left, stomp right; step right, stomp left; step left, stomp right twice. (Side, stomp, side, stomp, side, stomp)

21--24   Repeat action of measures 17--20. Teaching suggestions:

The stamps should be made close to the supporting foot. In teaching the dance, scatter the dancers in general space so they can move individually.

Korobushka (Russian)

Records: HLP 4028; CM 1162; WT 10005

Formation: Double circle, partner A's back to the center, with partners facing and both hands joined. A's left and B's right foot are free.

Directions:

Measures **Part I Action**

1--2   Take one schottische step away from the center (partner A moving forward, partner B backward) starting with A's left and B's right foot. (Out, 2, 3, hop)

3--4   Repeat the pattern of measures 1 and 2, reversing direction and footwork. (In, 2, 3, hop)

5--6   Repeat the pattern of measures 1 and 2, ending on the last count with a jump on both feet in place. (Out, 2, 3, jump)

7--8	Hop on the left foot, touching the right toes across in front of the left foot (count 1). Hop on the left foot, touching the right toes diagonally forward to the right (count 2). Jump on both feet in place, clicking the heels together (count 1), pause, and release the hands (count 2). (Across, apart, together)
Measures	**Part II Action**
9--10	Facing partner and beginning with the right foot, take one schottische step right, moving sideways away from partner. (Side, back, side, hop)
11--12	Facing and beginning with the left foot, take one schottische step left, returning to partner. (Side, back, side, hop)
13--14	Joining right hands with partner, balance forward and back: Step forward on the right foot (count 1), pause (count 2), rock back on the left foot in place (count 3), pause (count 4). (Forward, hop, back, hop)
15--16	Take four walking steps forward, starting with the right foot, and change places with partner. (Walk, 2, 3, 4)
17--24	Repeat the pattern of measures 9--16, returning to place.

Game Activity

Scooter Kickball

Supplies: A cageball, gym scooters for active players

Skill: Striking with various body parts

Each team is divided into active players (on scooters) and goal defenders. The active players are seated on the scooters, and the goal defenders are seated on the goal line, with feet extended. The object of the game is to kick the cageball over the goal line defended by the opposite team. The players are positioned as shown above.

The game starts with a face-off of two opposing players on scooters at the center of the court. The face-off is also used after a goal is scored. The active players on scooters propel the ball mainly with their feet. Touching the ball with the hands is a foul and results in a free kick by the opposition at the spot of the foul. A player also may use the head and body to stop and propel the ball.

The players defending the goal are seated on the goal line. They may not use their hands either, but use of the feet, body, and head is permitted. (If scoring seems too easy, then the defenders can be allowed to use their hands.) Defenders should be restricted to the seated position at the goal line; they are not permitted to enter the field of play to propel or stop the ball.

Teaching suggestions: If the sidelines are close to the walls of the gymnasium, out-of-bounds balls need not be called because the ball can rebound from the wall. The number of scooters determines the number of active players. The game works well if half of the players from each team are in the center on scooters and the other half are goal defenders. After a goal or after a stipulated time period, active players and goal defenders exchange places.

Some consideration should be made for glasses; otherwise they might be broken. Any active player who falls off a scooter should be required to seat herself again on the scooter before becoming eligible to propel the ball.

Variation: If there are enough scooters for everyone, the game can be played with rules similar to soccer. A more restricted goal (perhaps half of the end line) can be marked with standards. A goalie defends this area. All other players are active and can move to any spot on the floor. The floor space should be large enough to allow some freedom of play. Putting too many active players in a relatively small space causes jamming.

Touchdown

Supplies: A small object that can be concealed in the hand

Skills: Running, dodging

Two parallel lines about 60 ft apart are needed. Two teams face each other, each standing on one of the parallel lines. One team goes into a huddle, and the members decide which player is to carry an object to the opponents' goal line. The team moves out of the huddle and takes a position like a football team. On the charge signal "Hike," the players run toward the opponents' goal line, each player holding the hands closed as if carrying the object. On the charge signal, the opponents also run forward and tag the players. On being tagged, a player must stop immediately and open both hands to show whether or not he has the object. If the player carrying the object reaches the goal line without being tagged, she calls "Touchdown" and scores 6 points. The scoring team retains possession of the object and gets another try. If the player carrying the object is tagged in the center area, the object is given to the other team. They go into a huddle and try to run it across the field to score.

Chain Tag

Supplies: None

Skills: Running, dodging

Two parallel lines are established about 50 ft apart. The center is occupied by three players who form a chain with joined hands. The players with free hands on either end of the chain do the tagging. All other players line up on one of the parallel lines.

The players in the center call "Come," and children cross from one line to the other. The chain tries to tag the runners. Anyone caught joins the chain. When the chain becomes too long, it should be divided into several smaller chains.

Variation: <u>Catch of Fish</u>. The chain catches children by surrounding them like a fishing net. The runners cannot run under or through the links of the net.

Lesson Plans for Grades 5-6 - Week 29
Juggling Skills

Objectives:
To be able to juggle three scarves
To be able to juggle two balls
To participate in low organized games and contribute to the team outcome

Equipment Required:
Juggling scarves (3 for each student)
Different types of ball for juggling
Music and jump ropes for continuity drills

Instructional Activities	Teaching Hints

Introductory Activity -- Move, Exercise on Signal

Students do a locomotor movement, stop on signal and perform an exercise such as the following suggested activities: Push-Ups, Curl-Ups, Crab Kick, V-Ups, and Treadmills.

Use any locomotor movement. Students should get up and move as soon as they have completed the exercise.

Fitness Development Activity -- Continuity Drills

See Lesson Plan 12, p. 27-28 for a description of all the rope jumping steps. See text, p. 174-186 for descriptions of exercises.

Rope jumping—forward	30 seconds
Double Crab Kick	30 seconds
Rope jumping—backward	30 seconds
Knee Touch Curl-Up	30 seconds
Jump and turn body	30 seconds
Push-Ups	30 seconds
Rocker Step	30 seconds
Bend and Twist	30 seconds
Swing -Step forward	30 seconds
Side Flex	30 seconds
Free jumping	30 seconds

Relax and stretch for a short time.

Make a tape with music segments (25 seconds) alternated with silence segments (30 seconds). When the music is playing, students jump rope; when silence occurs, students do a flexibility and strength development exercise.

Exercises can be done in two-count fashion. Exercises are done when the leader says "Ready." The class answers "One-two" and performs a repetition.

Allow students to adjust the workload to their level. This implies resting if the rope jumping is too strenuous.

Lesson Focus -- Juggling Skills
Juggling with Scarves

Scarves are held by the fingertips near the center. To throw the scarf, it should be lifted and pulled into the air above eye level. Scarves are caught by clawing, a downward motion of the hand, and grabbing the scarf from above as it is falling.

Cascading—Cascading is the easiest pattern for juggling three objects. The following sequence can be used to learn this basic technique.

a. One scarf. Hold the scarf in the center. Quickly move the arm across the chest and toss the scarf with the palm out. Reach out with the other hand and catch the scarf in a straight-down motion (clawing). Toss the scarf with this hand using the motion and claw it with the opposite hand. Continue the tossing and clawing sequence over and over.

b. Two scarves and one hand. Hold the scarves with the fingertips in one hand. Toss the first scarf upward. As the first scarf reaches its zenith, toss the second scarf and catch the first one. Continue.

c. Two scarves and two hands. Hold a scarf with the fingertips of each hand. Toss the first one across the body as described above. Toss the second scarf across the body in the opposite direction.

d. Three-scarf cascading. A scarf is held in each hand by the fingertips as described above. The third scarf is held with the ring and little fingers against the palm of the hand. The first scarf to be thrown will be from the hand that is holding two scarves.

Reverse Cascading—Reverse cascading involves tossing the scarves from the waist level to the outside of the body and allowing the scarves to drop down the midline of the body.

a. One scarf.
b. Two scarves.
c. Three scarves.

Column Juggling—Column juggling is so named because the scarves move straight up and down as though they were inside a large pipe or column and do not cross the body.

Showering—Start with two scarves in the right hand and one in the other. Begin by throwing the first two scarves from the right hand. Toss the scarves in a large circle away from the midline of the body and overhead as high as possible. As soon as the second scarf is released, toss the scarf from the left to the right hand and throw it in the same path with the right hand. All scarves are caught with the left hand and passed to the right hand.

Juggling Challenges

a. While cascading, toss a scarf under one leg.
b. While cascading, toss a scarf from behind the back.
c. Instead of catching one of the scarves, blow it upward with a strong breath of air.
d. Begin cascading by tossing the first scarf into the air with a foot. Lay the scarf across the foot and kick it into the air.
e. Try juggling three scarves with one hand. Do not worry about establishing a pattern, just catch the lowest scarf each time. Try both regular and reverse cascading, as well as column juggling.
f. While doing column juggling, toss up one scarf, hold the other two and make a full turn. Resume juggling.
g. Try juggling more than three scarves (up to six) while facing a partner.
h. Juggle three scarves while standing beside a partner with inside arms around each other. This is easy to do since it is regular three-scarf cascading.

Juggling with Balls

Instructional Procedures

1. Juggling requires accurate, consistent tossing, and this should be the first emphasis. The tosses should be thrown to the same height on both sides of the body, about 2 to 2 feet upward and across the body, since the ball is tossed from one hand to the other. Practice tossing the ball parallel to the body; the most common problem in juggling is that the balls are tossed forward and the juggler has to move forward to catch them.
2. The fingers, not the palms, should be used in tossing and catching. Stress relaxed wrist action.
3. The student should look upward to watch the balls at the peak of their flight, rather than watching the hands. Focus on where the ball peaks, not the hands.
4. The balls should be caught about waist height and released a little above this level.
5. Two balls must be carried in the starting hand, and the art of releasing only one must be mastered.
6. Progression should be working successively with first one ball, then two balls, and finally three balls.

Recommended Progression for Cascading

1. Using one ball and one hand only, toss the ball upward (2 to 2 feet), and catch it with the same hand. Begin with the dominant hand, and later practice with the other. Toss quickly, with wrist action. Then handle the ball alternately with right and left hands, tossing from one hand to the other.
2. Now, with one ball in each hand, alternate tossing a ball upward and catching it in the same hand so that one ball is always in the air. Begin again with a ball in each hand. Toss across the body to the other hand. To keep the balls from colliding, toss under the incoming ball. After some expertise has been acquired, alternate the two kinds of tosses by doing a set number (four to six) of each before shifting to the other.
3. Hold two balls in the starting hand and one in the other. Toss one of the balls in the starting hand, toss the ball from the other hand, and then toss the third ball.

Game Activity

Bomb the Pins

Supplies: 8 to 12 bowling pins per team, 10 to 12 foam rubber balls
Skill: Throwing

A line is drawn across the center of the floor from wall to wall. This divides the floor into two courts, each of which is occupied by one team. Another line is drawn 25 ft from the centerline in each court. This is the line where each team spaces its bowling pins. Each team has at least five balls.

The object of the game is to knock over the other team's pins--not to throw at opponents. Players throw the balls back and forth, but the players cannot cross the centerline. Whenever a pin is knocked over by a ball or player (accidentally or not), that pin is removed. The team with the most pins standing at the end of the game is declared the winner. Out-of-bounds balls can be recovered but must be thrown from inside the court.

Variations: Pins can be reset instead of removed. Two scorers, one for each pin line, are needed. Rolling the balls is an excellent modification.

Pacman

Supplies: Markers in the shape of Pacman
Skills: Fleeing, reaction time

Three students are it and carry the Pacman marker. The remainder of the class is scattered throughout the area, standing on a floor line. Movement can only be made on a line.

Begin the game by placing the three taggers at the corners of the perimeter lines. Play is continuous; a player who is tagged takes the marker and becomes a new tagger. If a player leaves a line to escape being tagged, that player must secure a marker and become an additional tagger.

Lesson Plans for Grades 5-6 - Week 30
Relay Activities

Objectives:
To follow the rules when participating in relays
To accept winning gracefully
To understand the importance of cooperation when competing

Equipment Required:
Long jump ropes
Music tapes and individual jump ropes
for continuity drills
Cones and equipment for relays

Instructional Activities	Teaching Hints

Introductory Activity -- Hospital Tag

Every player is a tagger. Any player who is tagged must cover with one hand the body area that was touched. Students may be tagged twice but must be able to hold both tagged spots and keep moving. A student who is tagged three times must freeze. Restart the game when most of the students have been frozen.

All players are it. Don't wait for the last two players to be tagged. That approach keeps too many players standing. Start over often.

Fitness Development Activity -- Continuity Drills

See Lesson Plan 12, p. 27-28 for a description of all the rope jumping steps. See text, p. 174-186 for descriptions of exercises.

Rope jumping—forward	30 seconds
Double Crab Kick	35 seconds
Rope jumping—backward	30 seconds
Knee Touch Curl-Up	35 seconds
Jump and turn body	30 seconds
Push-Ups	35 seconds
Rocker Step	30 seconds
Bend and Twist	35 seconds
Swing -Step forward	30 seconds
Side Flex	35 seconds
Free jumping	30 seconds

Relax and stretch for a short time.

Make a tape with music segments (25 seconds) alternated with silence segments (30 seconds). When the music is playing, students jump rope; when silence occurs, students do a flexibility and strength development exercise.

Exercises can be done in two-count fashion. Exercises are done when the leader says "Ready." The class answers "One-two" and performs a repetition.

Allow students to adjust the workload to their level. This implies resting if the rope jumping is too strenuous.

Lesson Focus -- Relay Activities
Instructional Procedures for Relays

1. Teams should be restricted to four or five players. Too many on a team increases the amount of time spent waiting for a turn.
2. If teams have uneven numbers, some players on the smaller teams can run twice. All children on teams with fewer members must take a turn running twice; otherwise, the more skilled runners may always run and create an unfair advantage.
3. Teams should be changed regularly so that all youngsters have a chance to be on a winning team. Teachers should reserve the right to change team makeup as well as the order in which the students are placed on individual teams.
4. Placing less skilled players in the first or last position of the relay team will force these students to perform in front of the class and reveal to others that they are inferior. To avoid this situation, place less skilled students in the middle of the team. Discretion can be used when moving players to avoid labeling them as unskilled performers.
5. Infractions of the rules should be discussed. Relays are a social learning experience. Children are in a situation where they must conform to rules if the experience is going to be enjoyable for all students. This is an effective time to discuss how cooperation precedes competition; it is impossible to compete if players choose not to cooperate.
6. The finishing order must be determined properly. In giving instructions, teachers should be definite about the start, the turning point, and the finishing act.
7. A deceleration area should be delineated by a marker to prevent running into a wall. This turn-around and end area can be marked by cones, bowling pins, jump standards, or beanbags. With cones and bowling pins, knocking over the marker is a disqualification unless the runner resets it before proceeding.
8. Too much emphasis on winning makes the skilled resent losing and intimidates those of lesser ability. The idea of winning at any cost must be discussed and discouraged.
9. A trial run should always be made so that each team understands the procedures. If a new relay does not seem to have been started properly, stop the activity and review the instructions. Practice the relay first before embarking on a serious competitive run.
10. Traffic rules should be clear. In most cases, the way to the right governs. When runners go around the turning point, they do it from the right (counterclockwise), returning past the finish line on the right side. Some procedures to ensure a fair tagging off of the next runner should be instituted. Runners should not leave the restraining line before being tagged.

Relays

Introduce a variety of relays. The following are listed in sequence from easy to difficult. None of the relays require specialized sport skills (throwing, catching, etc.). This helps assure all students have the opportunity to contribute to their team's cooperative effort.

1. Carry-and-Fetch Relay

Players are in closed squad formation, with a hoop or circle positioned up to 30 feet in front of each team. The first runner on each team has a beanbag. On the command "Go," this player carries the beanbag forward and puts it inside the hoop, then returns and tags off the next runner. The second runner goes forward, picks up the beanbag, and hands it off to the third runner. One runner carries the beanbag forward and the next runner fetches it back. Different locomotor movements can be specified.

2. Attention Relay

The players on each team are facing forward in lane formation with team members about arms' distance apart. The distance between the teams should be about 10 feet. Two turning points are established for each team---one 10 feet in front of the team and the other 10 feet behind. Players are numbered consecutively from front to rear. The teacher calls, "Attention." All come to the attention position. The teacher calls out a number. The player on each team holding that number steps to the right, runs around the front and the back markers, and returns to place. The rest of the team runs in place. The first team to have all members at attention, including the returned runner, wins a point.

3. Pass and Squat Relay

One player (number 1) with a ball stands behind a line 10 feet in front of his teammates, who are in lane formation. Number 1 passes the ball to number 2, who returns the ball to number 1. As soon as he has returned the ball to number 1, number 2 squats down so that the throw can be made to number 3, and so on, down the file. When the last person in line receives the ball, she does not return it but carries it forward, straddling the members of her team, including number 1, who has taken a place at the head of the file. The player carrying the ball forward then acts as the passer. The race is over when the original number 1 player receives the ball in the back position and straddles the players to return to his original position.

4. Rescue Relay

Lane formation is used, with the first runner behind a line about 30 feet in front of the team. The first runner runs back to the team, takes the first player in line by the hand, and "rescues" him by leading him back to the 30-foot line. The player who has just been rescued then runs back to the team and gets the next player, and so on, until the last player has been conducted to the line. Some care must be taken that the front player in the file is behind the team line as the passing starts. After the straddling, repositioning the file is necessary. Each player should form a compact ball during the straddling activity.

5. Potato Relay

A small box about a foot square is placed 5 feet in front of each lane. Four 12-inch circles are drawn at 5-foot intervals beyond the box. This makes the last circle 25 feet from the starting point. Four blocks or beanbags are needed for each team. To start, the blocks are placed in the box in front of each team. The first runner goes to the box, takes a single block, and puts it into one of the circles. She repeats this performance until there is a block in each circle; then she tags off the second runner. This runner brings the blocks back to the box, one at a time, and tags off the third runner, who returns the blocks to the circles, and so on. Using a box to receive the blocks makes a definite target. When the blocks are taken to the circles, some rules must be made regarding placement. The blocks should be considered placed only when they are inside or touching a line. Blocks outside need to be replaced before the runner can continue. Paper plates or pie plates can be used instead of circles drawn on the floor.

6. Iceberg Relay

Teams are in lane formation, with each team having two rubber marking spots. The marks represent icebergs, and the task is to use the spots as stepping stones. Players race two at a time. One player is the stepper, and one moves the marking spots. The stepper may not touch the floor (fall in the ocean). The handler moves the marking spots to the turning point and then exchanges places with the stepper for the return trip. An alternative is to have the handler convey the stepper back to the starting point, give the marking spots to the next player at the head of the line, and then become the new stepper.

7. Jack Rabbit Relay (Jump Stick Relay)

Each runner carries a broomstick or wand, 1 meter in length, with both hands. A turning point is established about 30 feet in front of each lane. The race starts with the first player in line running forward around the turning point and back to the head of the line. In the meantime, the next player takes a short step to the right and gets ready to help with the stick. The runner with the stick returns on the left side and shifts the stick to the left hand. The second player reaches out with the right hand and takes the other end of the stick. The two then pass the stick under the others in the line, who must jump up to let it go through. When the stick has passed under all players, the original player releases the grip and remains at the end of the line. The second runner runs around the turning point and returns, and the next player in line helps with the stick, becoming the next runner when the stick has gone under all of the jumpers. Each player repeats until all have run.

To end the race properly takes a little doing. The simplest way is to call the race complete when the last runner crosses the line with the wand. Another way is to have the last runner, helped by the original first runner who by now has rotated to the front of the line, carry the wand under the team. The last runner releases the wand, and the first runner returns the wand to the head of the line.

Relaxation Activities

Relays are spirited. It might be useful to spend a few minutes relaxing.

1. In a supine position, practice some deep breathing with the eyes gently closed. Daydream while deep breathing about a favorite place.

2. Tense a muscle group, take a deep breath and hold it for 6 counts. Slowly exhale and relax the muscle group. Do the same with other muscle groups.

Lesson Plans for Grades 5-6 - Week 31
Track and Field Skills (1)

Objectives:
To understand how to stretch prior to strenuous activity
To recognize the wide range of individual differences among peers
To enjoy one-on-one competition in track and field activities

Equipment Required:
Stopwatches
Track and field equipment

Instructional Activities	Teaching Hints

Introductory and Fitness Development Activities-- Stretching and Jogging

Combine the introductory and fitness activities during the track and field unit. This will help students understand how to stretch and warm up for demanding activity such as track and field.

Jog	1-2 minutes
Standing Hip Bend	30 seconds
Sitting Stretch	30 seconds
Partner Rowing	60 seconds
Bear Hug (20 seconds each leg)	40 seconds
Side Flex (20 seconds each leg)	40 seconds
Trunk Twister	30 seconds
Jog	3-4 minutes

Emphasis should be on jogging and stretching to prepare for strenuous activity.

See text, p. 174-186 for descriptions of exercises.

Encourage smooth and controlled stretching. Hold each stretch for 6 to 10 seconds.

Lesson Focus -- Track and Field Skills (1)

Skills

Teach the following skills if students haven't learned them in earlier grades.

Standing Start

The standing start should be practiced, for this type of start has a variety of uses in physical education activities. Many children find it more comfortable than the sprinter's start. When practical, however, children should use the sprinter's start for track work. In the standing start, the feet should be in a comfortable half-stride position. An extremely long stride is to be avoided. The body leans forward so that the center of gravity is forward. The weight is on the toes, and the knees are flexed slightly. The arms can be down or hanging slightly back.

Sprinter's Start

"On your mark" position places the toe of the front foot from 4 to 12 inches behind the starting line. The thumb and first finger are just behind the line, with other fingers adding support. The knee of the rear leg is placed just opposite the front foot or ankle.

For the "Get set" position, the seat is raised so that it is nearly parallel to the ground. The knee of the rear leg is raised off the ground, and the shoulders are moved forward over the hands. The weight is evenly distributed over the hands and feet. The head is not raised, as the runner should be looking at a spot a few feet in front of the starting line.

On the "Go" signal, the runner pushes off sharply with both feet, with the front leg straightening as the back leg comes forward for a step. The body should rise gradually rather than pop up suddenly. The instructor should watch for a stumbling action on the first few steps. This results from too much weight resting on the hands in the "Get set" position.

Sprinting

In proper sprinting form, the body leans forward, with the arms swinging in opposition to the legs. The arms are bent at the elbows and swing from the shoulders in a forward and backward plane, not across the body. Forceful arm action aids sprinting. The knees are lifted sharply forward and upward and are brought down with a vigorous motion, followed by a forceful push from the toes.

The goal of track and field is self-improvement and developing proper techniques. Each student must accept responsibility for self-directed work and should be encouraged to try all activities.

The program should offer something for all---boys and girls, the highly skilled and the less skilled, and those with physical problems. Children with weight problems need particular attention. They must be stimulated and encouraged, since their participation will be minimal if little attention is paid to them. Special goals can be set for overweight children, and special events and goals can also be established for children with handicaps.

The long jump must be maintained properly. It should be filled with fresh sand of a coarse variety.

78

Baton Passing

The right hand to left hand method is the best choice for elementary school children as it is easy and offers a consistent method for passes. This pass allows the receiver to face the inside of the track while waiting to receive the baton in the left hand. The oncoming runner holds the baton in the right hand like a candle when passing it to a teammate. The receiver reaches back with the left hand, fingers pointing down and thumb to the inside, and begins to run as the runner advances to within 3 to 5 yards. The receiver grasps the baton and shifts it from the left to the right hand while moving. If the baton is dropped, it must be picked up, or the team is disqualified. An alternative way to receive the baton is to reach back with the hand facing up; however, the fingers-down method is considered more suitable for sprint relays.

Receivers can look over their shoulders to see the oncoming runner or can look forward in the direction of the run. Looking backward is called a visual pass and is slower than passing while looking forward (called a blind pass). However, there is a greater chance for error when the receiver is not looking backward and at the baton during the pass. The visual pass is recommended for elementary school children.

Distance Running

In distance running, as compared with sprinting, the body is more erect and the motion of the arms is less pronounced. Pace is an important consideration. Runners should try to concentrate on the qualities of lightness, ease, relaxation, and looseness. Good striding action, a slight body lean, and good head position are also important. Runners should be encouraged to strike the ground with the heel first and then push off with the toes.

If stop watches and tape measures are used, it is important to make them highly visible. Tie bright colored cord to them or anchor to cones to assure that they are not misplaced.

High Jumping - Scissors Jump

The scissors jump is by far the safest high jump and should be used for elementary school children when direct supervision is not available. For the scissors jump, the high-jump bar is approached from a slight angle. The takeoff is by the leg that is farther from the bar. The near leg is lifted and goes over, followed quickly in a looping movement by the rear leg. A good upward kick with the front leg, together with an upward thrust of the arms, is needed. The knees should be straightened at the highest point of the jump. The landing is made on the lead foot followed by the rear foot.

High-jump techniques are developed by practice. The bar should be at a height that offers challenge but allows concentration on technique rather than on height. Too much emphasis on competition for height quickly eliminates the poorer jumpers, who need the experience most.

Long Jump

For the running long jump, a short run is needed. The run should be timed so that the toes of the jumping foot contact the board in a natural stride. The jumper takes off from one foot and strives for height. The landing is made on both feet after the knees have been brought forward. The landing should be in a forward direction, not sideward.

A fair long jump takes off behind the scratch line. A foul (scratch) jump is called if the jumper steps beyond the scratch line or runs into or through the pit. Each contestant is given a certain number of trials (jumps). A scratch jump counts as a trial. Measurement is from the scratch line to the nearest point of touch.

Hop-Step-and-Jump

The hop-step-and-jump event is increasing in popularity, particularly because it is now included in Olympic competition. A takeoff board and a jumping pit are needed. The distance from the takeoff board to the pit should be one that even less skilled jumpers can make. The event begins with a run similar to that for the running long jump. The takeoff is with one foot, and the jumper must land on the same foot to complete the hop. He then takes a step followed by a jump. The event finishes like the long jump, with a landing on both feet (Figure 30.9). The pattern can be changed to begin with the left foot. A checkpoint should be used, as for the running long jump.

The jumper must not step over the takeoff board in the first hop, under penalty of fouling. Distance is measured from the front of the takeoff board to the closest place where the body touches. This is usually a mark made by one of the heels, but it could be a mark made by an arm or another part of the body if the jumper landed poorly and fell backward.

Station (Small Group) Instruction

The teacher should instruct at a different station each day. Start at the station that demands the most instruction. Set up a system of rotation that assures all stations will be covered during the unit.

Station 1

Starting and Sprinting

1. Front foot 4-12" behind line.
2. Thumb and first finger behind line, other fingers support.
3. Knee of other leg placed just opposite front foot.
4. On "get set," seat is raised, the down knee comes up a little, and the shoulders move forward over the hands.
5. On "go," push off sharply and take short, driving steps.

Make signs for each of the stations. The signs should include appropriate performance techniques, what is to be done at each station, and appropriate safety precautions.

Hop-Step-and-Jump (Triple Jump)
1. Important to get the sequence and rhythm first, then later try for distance.
2. Sprinting.

Station 2
Running High Jump
1. Keep stretch rope low enough so all can practice.
2. Approach at 45°
3. Good kick-up and arm action.
Baton Passing
1. Decide on method of passing.
2. Incoming runner passes with left hand to right hand of receiver.
3. After receiving, change to the left hand.
4. Estimate how fast to take off with respect to the incoming runner.

Station 3
Running Long Jump
1. Decide on jumping foot.
2. Establish check point.
3. Control last four steps.
4. Seek height.
Standing Long Jump or Shuttle Relays

Station 4
Hurdling
1. At beginning, use one or two hurdles.
2. Leading foot is directly forward.
Practice Striding for Distance Running
1. Work on pace.
2. Easy, relaxed strides.

The goal of the program should be to allow students to develop at their own rate. The instructor needs to be perceptive enough to determine whether students are working too hard or too little. Special attention must be given to those who appear disinterested, dejected, emotionally upset, or withdrawn.

Game Activity

Circular (Pursuit) Relays

Circular relays make use of the regular circular track. The baton exchange technique is important, and practice is needed. On a 220-yd or 200-m track, relays can be organized in a number of ways, depending on how many runners are spaced for one lap. Four runners can do a lap, each running one quarter of the way; two can do a lap, each running one half of the distance; or each runner can complete a whole lap. In these races, each member of the relay team runs the same distance. Relays can also be organized so that members run different distances.

Shuttle Relays

Since children are running toward each other, one great difficulty in running shuttle relays is control of the exchange. In the excitement, the next runner may leave too early, and the tag or exchange is then made ahead of the restraining line. A high-jump standard or cone can be used to prevent early exchanges. The next runner awaits the tag with an arm around the standard or a hand on a cone.

One on One Contests

Allow students to find a friend and have a number of personal contests in track and field events such as sprints, hurdling, high jump, and standing long jump.

Lesson Plans for Grades 5-6 - Week 32
Track and Field Skills (2)

Objectives:
To understand how to stretch prior to strenuous activity
To recognize the wide range of individual differences among peers
To enjoy one-on-one competition in track and field activities

Equipment Required:
Stopwatches
Track and field equipment

Instructional Activities	Teaching Hints

Introductory and Fitness Development Activities—Stretching and Jogging

Combine the introductory and fitness activities during the track and field unit. This will help students understand how to stretch and warm up for demanding activity such as track and field.

Jog	1-2 minutes	
Standing Hip Bend	30 seconds	
Sitting Stretch	30 seconds	
Partner Rowing	60 seconds	
Bear Hug (20 seconds each leg)	40 seconds	
Side Flex (20 seconds each leg)	40 seconds	
Trunk Twister	30 seconds	
Jog	3-4 minutes	

Emphasis should be on jogging and stretching to prepare for strenuous activity.

See text, p. 174-186 for descriptions of exercises.

Encourage smooth and controlled stretching. Hold each stretch for 6 to 10 seconds.

Lesson Focus -- Track and Field Skills (2)

Skills

Introduce the following skills before proceeding to small group instruction.

Striding

In distance running, as compared with sprinting, the body is more erect and the motion of the arms is less pronounced. Pace is an important consideration. Runners should try to concentrate on the qualities of lightness, ease, relaxation, and looseness. Good striding action, a slight body lean, and good head position are also important. Runners should be encouraged to strike the ground with the heel first and then push off with the toes

Hurdling

Several key points govern good hurdling technique. The runner should adjust his stepping pattern so that the takeoff foot is planted 3 to 5 feet from the hurdle. The lead foot is extended straight forward over the hurdle; the rear (trailing) leg is bent, with the knee to the side. The lead foot reaches for the ground, quickly followed by the trailing leg. The hurdler should avoid floating over the hurdle. Body lean is necessary. A hurdler may lead with the same foot over consecutive hurdles or may alternate the leading foot. Some hurdlers like to thrust both arms forward instead of a single arm. A consistent step pattern should be developed.

Wands supported on blocks or cones can also be used as hurdles. Hurdles should begin at about 12 inches in height and increase to 18 inches. They should be placed about 25 feet apart.

Station (Small Group) Instruction

Review skills that were taught last week, if necessary. The teacher should instruct at a different station each day. Start at the station that demands the most instruction. Set up a system of rotation that assures all stations will be covered during the unit. Allow youngsters to work with a partner of somewhat equal ability. At each station, set out signs that tell students what they are to practice and list key performance points.

Station 1

Sprinting - Partners time each other over different distances.
1. 60 yard distance
2. 75 yard distance
3. Record best performance
Hop-Step-and-Jump - Partners take turns practicing the hop, step, and jump.
1. Three trials
2. Record best performance

Station 2

High Jump - Partners practice the scissors jump
1. Each jump begins at a height they desire. If the jump is made, they can dictate how much to raise the height.
2. Three trials.
3. Record best performance

Baton Passing - Practice passing the baton with partner while waiting for high jump turn.

Station 3

Running Long Jump - Partners take turns performing the running long jump.
1. Three trials.
2. Record best performance

Shuttle Relays - Partners practice with another set of partners, about 20 yards apart and facing each other. See below for a description of shuttle relays.

Station 4

Hurdling - Partners time each other over a three hurdle course.
1. Set up 60-yard hurdle course.
2. Two trials.
3. Record best performance.

Striding Practice - Striding practice can be done while waiting for turns on the hurdles.

Game Activity

Circular (Pursuit) Relays

Circular relays make use of the regular circular track. The baton exchange technique is important, and practice is needed. On a 220-yd or 200-m track, relays can be organized in a number of ways, depending on how many runners are spaced for one lap. Four runners can do a lap, each running one quarter of the way; two can do a lap, each running one half of the distance; or each runner can complete a whole lap. In these races, each member of the relay team runs the same distance. Relays can also be organized so that members run different distances.

Shuttle Relays

Since children are running toward each other, one great difficulty in running shuttle relays is control of the exchange. In the excitement, the next runner may leave too early, and the tag or exchange is then made ahead of the restraining line. A high-jump standard or cone can be used to prevent early exchanges. The next runner awaits the tag with an arm around the standard or a hand on a cone.

One on One Contests

Allow students to find a friend and have a number of personal contests in track and field events such as sprints, hurdling, high jump, and standing long jump.

Lesson Plans for Grades 5-6 - Week 33
Track and Field Skills (3)

Objectives:
To understand how to stretch prior to strenuous activity
To recognize the wide range of individual differences among peers
To enjoy one-on-one competition in track and field activities

Equipment Required:
Stopwatches
Track and field equipment

Instructional Activities	Teaching Hints

Introductory and Fitness Development Activities-- Stretching and Jogging

Combine the introductory and fitness activities during the track and field unit. This will help students understand how to stretch and warm up for demanding activity such as track and field.		Emphasis should be on jogging and stretching to prepare for strenuous activity.
Jog	1-2 minutes	
Standing Hip Bend	30 seconds	See text, p. 174-186 for descriptions of
Sitting Stretch	30 seconds	exercises.
Partner Rowing	60 seconds	
Bear Hug (20 seconds each leg)	40 seconds	Encourage smooth and controlled
Side Flex (20 seconds each leg)	40 seconds	stretching. Hold each stretch for 6 to 10
Trunk Twister	30 seconds	seconds.
Jog	3-4 minutes	

Lesson Focus -- Track and Field Skills (3)

Track and Field Skills
1. Utilize the last week of this unit to conduct a track and field meet. The same rotation plan and groups of students started the previous two weeks can be continued for the meet.
2. Utilize the same stations, events, number of trials and scoring procedures outlined in last week's track and field lesson.

Game Activity

Circular (Pursuit) Relays
   Circular relays make use of the regular circular track. The baton exchange technique is important, and practice is needed. On a 220-yd or 200-m track, relays can be organized in a number of ways, depending on how many runners are spaced for one lap. Four runners can do a lap, each running one quarter of the way; two can do a lap, each running one half of the distance; or each runner can complete a whole lap. In these races, each member of the relay team runs the same distance. Relays can also be organized so that members run different distances.

Shuttle Relays
   Since children are running toward each other, one great difficulty in running shuttle relays is control of the exchange. In the excitement, the next runner may leave too early, and the tag or exchange is then made ahead of the restraining line. A high-jump standard or cone can be used to prevent early exchanges. The next runner awaits the tag with an arm around the standard or a hand on a cone.

One on One Contests
   Allow students to find a friend and have a number of personal contests in track and field events such as sprints, hurdling, high jump, and standing long jump.

Lesson Plans for Grades 5-6 - Week 34
Long-Rope Jumping Skills

Objectives:
To prepare one's body for strenuous activity
To jump a rope turned by others
To know the difference in long-rope jumping between entering front and back doors
To understand how to enter and exit in double dutch rope jumping

Equipment Required:
Squad leader exercises task cards
Music for exercises and rope jumping
6-12 long jump ropes (16 ft long)
Cageball and 12-15 throwing balls for game

Instructional Activities	Teaching Hints

Introductory Activity -- Personal Choice

Students select any type of activity they wish to use to warm up. They may use one they have previously learned in class, or they may create one of their own. Emphasis should be on a balanced approach that works all major muscle groups.

If desired, students can work with a partner and share ideas with each other for desired activities.

Fitness Development Activity -- Squad Leader Exercises with Task Cards

Place the names of exercises on task cards. See text, p. 174-186 for descriptions of exercises.

Sitting Stretch
Push-Up challenges
Body Circles
Jumping Jack variations
Crab Kick combinations
Abdominal challenges
Treadmills
Toe Touchers
Leg Extensions

If there is a delay in starting an exercise, the squad should walk or jog.

The class is divided into groups of four to five students. Each group is given a task card that lists eight to ten exercises. One of the group members begins as the leader and leads the group through an exercise. Each time an exercise is completed, the card is passed to a new leader.

Use alternating intervals of music to signal exercising (30 seconds) with silence (5-8 seconds) to indicate passing the card.

Lesson Focus -- Long-Rope Jumping Skills

Single Long-Rope Activities

1. Review previously learned jumping skills. Teach the difference between entering front and back doors. Front door means entering from the side where the rope is turning forward and toward the jumper after it reaches its peak. Back door means entering from the side where the rope is turning backward and away from the jumper. To enter front door, the jumper follows the rope in and jumps when it completes the turn. To enter back door, the jumper waits until the rope reaches its peak and moves in as the rope moves downward. Learning to enter at an angle is usually easier, but any path that is comfortable is acceptable.
2. Have more than one youngster jump at a time. Students can enter in pairs or triplets.
3. Jump while holding a beanbag or playground ball between the knees.
4. While turning rope, rotate under the rope and jump. Continue jumping and rotate back to the turning position.
5. Play catch with a playground ball while jumping.
6. Do the Egg Beater: Two or more long ropes are turned simultaneously. The ropes are aligned perpendicular to each other; the jumper jumps the rope where they cross.
7. Try combinations of three or four ropes turning. The ropes are aligned parallel to each other and students jump and move through to the next rope.

Four children is an appropriate group size for practicing long-rope skills. Two members of the group turn the rope while the others practice jumping. A plan for rotating turners is important so that all children receive similar amounts of practice jumping.

Long ropes should be 16 feet in length.

Instructional cues to teach long-rope jumping skills are:
a. Turn the rope with the forearm.
b. Lock the wrist and keep the thumb up while turning.
c. Stand perpendicular to the rope.
d. Barely touch the floor with the turning rope.
e. Don't cross the midline of the body with the forearm while turning the rope.
f. Jump on the balls of the feet.

Double Dutch (two ropes) Activities

1. Teach entering and exiting. Basic jump on both feet. Land on the balls of the feet, keeping ankles and knees together with hands across the stomach.
   Entering: When entering, stand beside a turner and run into the ropes when the back rope (farther from the jumper) touches the floor. Turners should be taught to say "Go" each time the back rope touches the floor.
   Exiting: Exit the ropes by facing and jumping toward one turner and exiting immediately after jumping. The exit should be made as close to the turner's shoulder as possible.
2. Jogging Step. Run in place with a jogging step. Increase the challenge by circling while jogging.
3. Scissors Jump. Jump to a stride position with the left foot forward and the right foot back about 8 inches apart. Each jump requires reversing the position of the feet.
4. Straddle Jump. Jump to the straddle position and return to closed position. Try a Straddle Cross Jump by crossing the legs on return to the closed position. The straddle jumps should be performed facing away from the turners.
5. Turnaround. Circle left or right using the basic jump. Begin circling slowly at first and then increase speed. To increase the challenge, try the turnaround on one foot.
6. Hot Peppers. Use the Jogging Step and gradually increase the speed of the ropes.
7. Half Turn. Perform a half turn with each jump. Remember to lead the turn with the head and shoulders.
8. Ball Tossing. Toss and catch a playground ball while jumping.
9. Individual Rope Jumping. Enter Double Dutch with an individual rope and jump. Face the turner and decrease the length of the individual jump rope.

Arm positions and turning motions are similar to turning a single long rope. In short, keep the upper arm stationary, rotate at the elbow with locked wrist, and keep the thumb up. Avoid crossing the midline of the body, and establish an even cadence. Rotate the hands inward toward the midline of the body (right forearm counterclockwise and left forearm clockwise).

Double Dutch turning takes considerable practice. Take time to teach it as a skill that is necessary for successful jumping experiences.

Students should concentrate on the sound of the ropes hitting the floor so that they make an even and rhythmic beat.

Concentrate on jumping in the center of the ropes facing a turner. Use white shoe polish to mark a jumping target.

Game Activity

Cageball Target Throw

Supplies: A cageball (18- to 30-in.), 12 to 15 smaller balls of various sizes
Skill: Throwing

An area about 20 ft wide is marked across the center of the playing area, with a cageball in the center. The object of the game is to throw the smaller balls against the cageball, thus forcing it across the line in front of the other team. Players may come up to the line to throw, but they may not throw while inside the cageball area. A player may enter the area, however, to recover a ball. No one is to touch the cageball at any time, nor may the cageball be pushed by a ball in the hands of a player.

Teaching suggestion: If the cageball seems to roll too easily, it should be deflated slightly. The throwing balls can be of almost any size--soccer balls, volleyballs, playground balls, or whatever.

Variation: Two rovers, one from each team, can occupy the center area to retrieve balls. These players cannot block throws or prevent a ball from hitting the target. They are there for the sole purpose of retrieving balls for their team.

Sunday

Supplies: None
Skills: Running, dodging

Two parallel lines are drawn about 50 ft apart. One player is it and stands in the center of the area between the two lines. All of the other children are on one of the two lines. The object is to cross to the other line without being tagged and without making a false start.

Each line player stands with her front foot on the line. The line players must run across the line immediately when the tagger calls "Sunday." Anyone who does not run immediately is considered caught. The tagger can call other days of the week to confuse the runners. No player may make a start if another day of the week is called. The tagger must be careful to pronounce "Monday" in such a way that it cannot be confused with "Sunday." If confusion does occur, "Monday" can be eliminated from the signals for the false start.

Teaching suggestion: "Making a start" must be defined clearly. To begin, it can be defined as a player moving either foot. Later, when children get better at the game, a forward movement of the body can constitute a start.

Lesson Plans for Grades 5-6 - Week 35
Softball Skills (1)

Objectives:
To throw and catch a softball
To hit a softball
To be able to field softball grounders and fly balls
To know the basic rules of softball
To understand the roles of different positions in softball

Equipment Required:
Music and squad leader exercise task cards
Station 1: Two batting tees
Station 2: Two balls
Station 3: Four bases and 4 balls
Station 4: Two balls and 2 bats

Instructional Activities	Teaching Hints

Introductory Activity -- Personal Choice

Students select any type of activity they wish to use to warm up. They may use one they have previously learned in class, or they may create one of their own. Emphasis should be on a balanced approach that works all major muscle groups.

If desired, students can work with a partner and share ideas with each other for desired activities.

Fitness Development Activity -- Squad Leader Exercises with Task Cards

Place the names of exercises on task cards. See text, p. 174-186 for descriptions of exercises.

Sitting Stretch
Push-Up challenges
Body Circles
Jumping Jack variations
Crab Kick combinations
Abdominal challenges
Treadmills
Toe Touchers
Leg Extensions

If there is a delay in starting an exercise, the squad should walk or jog.

The class is divided into groups of four to five students. Each group is given a task card that lists eight to ten exercises. One of the group members begins as the leader and leads the group through an exercise. Each time an exercise is completed, the card is passed to a new leader.

Use alternating intervals of music to signal exercising (30 seconds) with silence (5-8 seconds) to indicate passing the card.

Lesson Focus -- Softball Skills (1)

Skills
Practice the following skills:

1. Overhand Throw

In preparation for throwing, the child secures a firm grip on the ball, raises the throwing arm to shoulder height, and brings the elbow back. For the overhand throw, the hand with the ball is then brought back over the head so that it is well behind the shoulder at about shoulder height. The left side of the body is turned in the direction of the throw, and the left arm is raised in front of the body. The weight is on the back (right) foot, with the left foot advanced and the toe touching the ground. The arm comes forward with the elbow leading, and the ball is thrown with a downward snap of the wrist. The body weight is brought forward into the throw, shifting to the front foot. There should be good follow-through so that the palm of the throwing hand faces the ground at completion of the throw. The eyes should be on the target throughout, and the arm should be kept free and loose during the throw.

2. Pitching

Official rules call for the pitcher to have both feet in contact with the pitcher's rubber, but few elementary schools possess a rubber. Instead, the pitcher can stand with both feet about even, facing the batter, and holding the ball momentarily in front with both hands. The pitcher takes one hand from the ball, extends the right arm forward, and brings it back in a pendulum swing, positioning the ball well behind the body. A normal stride taken toward the batter with the left foot begins the throwing sequence for a right-handed pitcher. The arm is brought forward with an underhanded slingshot motion, and the weight is transferred to the leading foot. Only one step is permitted.

Whiffle balls and plastic bats are a much safer alternative for children this age. It is easier for them to swing plastic bats and the fear of getting hit by a softball will not be an issue.

Instructional cues for **throwing** are:
1. Place the throwing arm side of the body away from the target.
2. Step toward the target with the foot opposite the throwing hand.
3. Bend and raise the arm at the elbow. Lead with the elbow.

Instructional cues for **pitching** are:
1. Face the plate.
2. Keep your eyes on the target.
3. Swing the pitching arm backward and step forward.

3. Fielding Grounders

To field a grounder, the fielder should move as quickly as possible into the path of the ball and then move forward and play the ball on a good hop. The eyes must be kept on the ball, following it into the hands or glove. The feet are spread, the seat is kept down, and the hands are carried low and in front. The weight is on the balls of the feet or on the toes, and the knees are bent to lower the body. As the ball is caught, the fielder straightens up, takes a step in the direction of the throw, and makes the throw.

4. Batting (Right-Handed)

The batter stands with the left side of the body toward the pitcher. The feet are spread and the weight is on both feet. The body should be facing the plate. The bat is held with the trademark up, and the left hand grasps the bat lower than the right. The bat is held over the right shoulder, pointing both back and up. The elbows are away from the body. The swing begins with a hip roll and a short step forward in the direction of the pitcher. The bat is then swung level with the ground at the height of the pitch. The eyes are kept on the ball until it is hit. After the hit, there must be good follow-through.

Instructional cues for **fielding** are:
1. Move into line with the path of the ball.
2. Give when catching the ball.
3. Use the glove to absorb the force of the ball.
4. For grounders, keep the head down and watch the ball move into the glove.

Instructional cues for **batting** are:
1. Keep the hands together.
2. Swing the bat horizontally.
3. Swing through the ball.
4. Hold the bat off the shoulder.
5. Watch the ball hit the bat.

Station (Small Group) Instruction

The teacher should instruct at a different station each day. Start at the station that demands the most instruction. Set up a system of rotation that assures all stations will be covered during the unit.

Station 1 - Batting

Use a batting tee. For each station, two tees are needed, with a bat and at least two balls for each tee. Three to five children are assigned to each tee. There should be a batter, a catcher to handle incoming balls, and fielders. When only three children are in a unit, the catcher should be eliminated. Each batter is allowed a certain number of swings before rotating to the field. The catcher becomes the next batter, and a fielder moves up to catcher.

Hitters should avoid the following: lifting the front foot high off the ground, stepping back with the rear foot, or bending forward.

Station 2 - Throwing and Catching

Work with a partner and practice some of the following throwing drills:
a. Throw back and forth, practicing various throws.
b. gradually increase the distance of the throws.
c. focus on accuracy; if the throws are not caught, reduce the distance between players

Stand about 7 to 10 yards apart when practicing throwing.

For youngsters who are afraid of the ball, use a whiffle ball.

Station 3 - Pitching

Students find a partner and pitch and catch with each other. Set out a number of bases at each station so pitchers can pitch and catch using a base as a target (home plate).
a. Pitch to another player over a plate.
b. Call balls and strikes. One player is the pitcher, the second is the catcher, and the third is the umpire. A fourth player can be a stationary batter to provide a more realistic pitching target.

Face the batter, both feet on the rubber and the ball held in front with both hands. One step is allowed, and the ball must be delivered on that step.
Ball must be pitched underhanded.
No motion or fake toward the plate can be made without delivering the ball.

Station 4 - Fielding

Players find a partner and practice throwing grounders and fly balls to each other.
a. One partner throws a grounder or fly ball, the other partner fields the ball and throws it back to the other. Reverse roles.
b. Do the same thing above except use a bat to hit the balls.

Show form for high and low catch.

Move into the path of the ball.

Game Activity

Batter Ball

Supplies: A softball, a bat, a mask
Skills: Slow pitching, hitting, fielding, catching flies

Batter Ball involves batting and fielding but no base running. It is much like batting practice but adds the element of competition. A line is drawn directly from first to third base. This is the balk line over which a batted ball must travel to be fielded. Another line is drawn from a point on the foul line 3 ft behind third base to a point 5 ft behind second base and in line with home plate. Another line connects this point with a point on the other baseline 3 ft behind first base.

Each batter is given three pitches by a member of his own team to hit the ball into fair territory across the balk line. The pitcher may stop any ground ball before it crosses the balk line. The batter then gets another turn at bat.

Scoring is as follows:

1. A successful grounder scores 1 point. A grounder is successful when an infielder fails to handle it cleanly within the infield area. Only one player may field the ball. If the ball is fielded properly, the batter is out.

2. A line drive in the infield area is worth 1 point if not caught. It can be handled for an out on any bounce. Any line drive caught on the fly is also an out.

3. A fly ball in the infield area scores 1 point if not caught. For an out, the ball must be caught legally by the first person touching it.

4. A two-bagger scores 2 points. Any fly ball, line drive or not, that lands fairly in the outfield area without being caught scores 2 points. If it is caught, the batter is out.

5. A home run scores 3 points. Any fly ball driven over the head of the farthest outfielder in that area scores a home run.

Three outs can constitute an inning, or all batters can be allowed one turn at bat and then the team changes to the field. A new set of infielders should be in place for each inning. The old set goes to the outfield. Pitchers should be limited to one inning. They also take a turn at bat.

Teaching suggestion: Many games of this type require special fields, either rectangular or narrowly angled. This game was selected because it uses the regular softball field with the added lines. The lines can be drawn with a stick or can be marked using regular marking methods.

The pitcher has to decide whether he should stop the ball. If the ball goes beyond the restraining line, it is in play even if he touched it.

Variations: Batter Ball can be modified for use as a station in rotational teaching, with the emphasis on individual batting and squad organization. One member of the squad would be at bat and would get a definite number of chances (e.g., five) to score. She keeps her own point total. The other squad members occupy the necessary game positions.

Tee Ball

Supplies: A softball, a bat, a batting tee

Skills: Most softball skills (except pitching and stealing bases), hitting a ball from a tee

This game is an excellent variation of softball and is played under softball rules with the following exceptions.

1. Instead of hitting a pitched ball, the batter hits the ball from a tee. The catcher places the ball on the tee. After the batter hits the ball, the play is the same as in regular softball. With no pitching, there is no stealing. A runner stays on the base until the ball is hit by the batter.

2. A fielder occupies the position normally held by the pitcher. The primary duty of this fielder is to field bunts and ground balls and to back up the infielders on throws.

Teams can play regular innings for three outs or change to the field after each player has had a turn at bat.

Teaching suggestions: A tee can be purchased or made from a radiator hose. If the tee is not adjustable, three different sizes should be available. The batter should take a position far enough behind the tee so that, in stepping forward to swing, she will hit the ball slightly in front of her.

Tee Ball has many advantages. There are no strikeouts, every child hits the ball, there is no dueling between pitcher and batter, and fielding opportunities abound.

Scrub (Work-Up)

Supplies: A softball, a bat

Skills: Most softball skills

The predominant feature of Scrub is the rotation of the players. The game is played with regular softball rules, with each individual more or less playing for herself. There are at least two batters, generally three. A catcher, pitcher, and first-base player are essential. The remaining players assume the other positions. Whenever the batter is out, she goes to a position in right field. All other players move up one position, with the catcher becoming the batter. The first-base player becomes the pitcher, the pitcher moves to catcher, and all others move up one place.

Variation: If a fly ball is caught, the fielder and batter exchange positions.

Lesson Plans for Grades 5-6 - Week 36
Softball Skills (2)

Objectives:
To throw and catch a softball
To hit a softball
To be able to field softball grounders and fly balls
To know the basic rules of softball
To understand the roles of different positions in softball

Equipment Required:
Music and squad leader exercise task cards
Station 1: One bats and 4 balls
Station 2: Three home plates and 3 balls
Station 3: Four bases, ball and bat
Station 4: One bat and 4 balls

Instructional Activities	Teaching Hints

Introductory Activity -- Personal Choice

Students select any type of activity they wish to use to warm up. They may use one they have previously learned in class, or they may create one of their own. Emphasis should be on a balanced approach that works all major muscle groups.

If desired, students can work with a partner and share ideas with each other for desired activities.

Fitness Development Activity -- Squad Leader Exercises with Task Cards

Place the names of exercises on task cards. See text, p. 174-186 for descriptions of exercises.

Sitting Stretch
Push-Up challenges
Body Circles
Jumping Jack variations
Crab Kick combinations
Abdominal challenges
Treadmills
Toe Touchers
Leg Extensions

If there is a delay in starting an exercise, the squad should walk or jog.

The class is divided into groups of four to five students. Each group is given a task card that lists eight to ten exercises. One of the group members begins as the leader and leads the group through an exercise. Each time an exercise is completed, the card is passed to a new leader.

Use alternating intervals of music to signal exercising (30 seconds) with silence (5-8 seconds) to indicate passing the card.

Lesson Focus -- Softball Skills (2)

Skills
Review skills learned last week:
1. Overhand Throw
2. Pitching
3. Fielding Grounders
4. Batting
Introduce new skills:
Fielding Fly Balls
    There are two ways to catch a fly ball. For a low ball, the fielder keeps the fingers together and forms a basket with the hands. For a higher ball, the thumbs are together, and the ball is caught in front of the chin. The fielder should give with the hands, and care must be taken with a spinning ball to squeeze the hands sufficiently to stop the spinning. The eye is on the ball continually until it hits the glove or hands. The knees are flexed slightly when receiving and aid in giving when the ball is caught.

Station (Small Group) Instruction
The teacher should instruct at a different station each day. Start at the station that demands the most instruction. Set up a system of rotation that assures all stations will be covered during the unit.

Station 1 - Outfield Practice
One player in the group hits fly balls. The others field and practice using the sure stop when the ball is not caught on the fly. Rotate batters after 8 fly balls have been hit.

Whiffle balls and plastic bats are a much safer alternative for children this age. It is easier for them to swing plastic bats and the fear of getting hit by a softball will not be an issue.

Sure Stop for Outfield Balls
    To keep the ball from going through the hands and thus allowing extra bases, the outfielder can use the body as a barrier. The fielder turns half right and lowers one knee to the ground at the point toward which the ball is traveling. The hands catch the rolling ball, but if it is missed, the body will generally stop the ball.

If youngsters are not able to hit the ball, they can catch and throw it to the fielders.

Station 2 - Pitching and Umpiring

Students find a partner and pitch and catch with each other. Set out a number of bases at each station so pitchers can pitch and catch using a base as a target (home plate).

1. Pitch to another player over a plate.
2. Call balls and strikes. One player is the pitcher, the second is the catcher, and the third is the umpire. A fourth player can be a stationary batter to provide a more realistic pitching target.

When umpiring, strikes are called by raising the right hand and balls require raising the left hand.

Station 3 - Infield Practice

1. Throw around the bases clockwise and counterclockwise.
2. Throw grounders to infielders and make the play at first. After each play, throw around the infield.
3. If students have enough skill, bat the ball to the infielders in turn.

While having infield practice, one person at the station can run the bases and try to complete a circuit around the bases before the ball does.

Station 4 - Batting Practice

Each batter takes six swings and then rotates to the field. Catcher becomes batter and pitcher moves up to catcher.

Have more than one ball at the stations so the pitching can continue when a ball is hit or not caught.

Game Activity

Scrub (Work-Up)

See Softball Skills, Lesson 1 (p. 88) for a complete game description.

Slow-Pitch Softball

Supplies: A softball, a bat

Skills: Most softball skills

The major difference between regular softball and Slow-Pitch Softball is in the pitching, but there are other modifications to the game as well. With slower pitching, there is more hitting and thus more action on the bases and in the field. Outfielders are an important part of the game, because many long drives are hit. Rule changes from the game of official softball are as follows.

1. The pitch must be a slow pitch. Any other pitch is illegal and is called a ball. The pitch must be slow, with an arc of 1 ft. It must not rise over 10 ft from the ground, however. Its legality depends on the umpire's call.

2. There are ten players instead of nine. The extra one, called the roving fielder, plays in the outfield and handles line drives hit just over the infielders.

3. The batter must take a full swing at the ball and is out if he chops at the ball or bunts.

4. If the batter is hit by a pitched ball, she is not entitled to first base. The pitch is merely called a ball. Otherwise, balls and strikes are called as in softball.

5. The runner must hold base until the pitch has reached or passed home plate. No stealing is permitted.

Teaching suggestion: Shortening the pitching distance somewhat may be desirable. Much of the success of the game depends on the pitcher's ability to get the ball over the plate.

Babe Ruth Ball

Supplies: A bat, a ball, four cones or other markers

Skills: Batting, pitching, fielding

The three outfield zones--left, center, and right field--are separated by four cones. It is helpful if foul lines have been drawn, but cones can define them The batter calls the field to which he intends to hit. The pitcher throws controlled pitches so that the batter can hit easily. The batter remains in position as long as he hits to the designated field. Field choices must be rotated. The batter gets only one swing to make a successful hit. He may allow a ball to go by, but if he swings, it counts as a try. There is no base running. Players rotate.

Teaching suggestions: Children play this game informally on sandlots with a variety of rules. Some possibilities to consider are these: What happens when a fly ball is caught? What limitations should be made on hitting easy grounders? Let the players decide about these points and others not covered by the stated rules.

Three-Team Softball

Supplies: A mask, a ball, a bat

Skills: All softball skills

Three-Team Softball works well with 12 players, a number considered too few to divide into two effective fielding teams. The players are instead divided into three teams. The rules of softball apply, with the following exceptions.

1. One team is at bat, one team covers the infield (including the catcher), and the third team provides the outfielders and the pitcher.

2. The team at bat must bat in a definite order. This means that because of the small number of batters on each side, instances can occur when the person due to bat is on base. To take a turn at bat, the runner must be replaced by a player not on base.

3. After three outs, the teams rotate, with the outfield moving to the infield, the infield taking a turn at bat, and the batters going to the outfield.

4. An inning is over when all three teams have batted.

5. The pitcher should be limited to pitching one inning only. A player may repeat as pitcher only after all members of his team have had a chance to pitch.

NOTES

NOTES

NOTES

NOTES

NOTES